To Rich,

Pilgrimage to our Father's House

Blessings,

Brendan

ISBN: 979-8-631318-62-5

Pilgrimage to our Father's House

*Continuing to draw wellsprings of love
from the Heart of Jesus
through the power of the Holy Spirit*

A Gospel Approach and Experience

H. B. Williams

CONTENTS

INTRODUCTION

We are living in a painful and difficult time in the Church. We see millions falling away from the faith. Even among those who attend Church, we find only about twenty-five percent who believe in the doctrine of the Real Presence. We are baffled by some of the strange twists and departures from essential teachings in matters of faith and morals. And this is not coming from a scattered group of renegades, it is emerging from some of the heart of the Church's spiritual leaders, all the way to the top. We have, for example, some of the German Hierarchy calling for a re-writing of the Catechism of the Catholic Church, so as to legitimize issues and trends that are now expressly forbidden by the doctrine of faith.

But let us not be overwhelmed or lose faith. Bishop Fulton Sheen, we hope, will soon be honored with sainthood. He once met with the well-known convert to the Catholic Church, Malcolm Muggeridge. Their conversation, among many issues, centered on the demise of Christian civilization. Bishop Sheen's final comment to his guest was surely one to remember: "Christendom is over but not Christ."

Let us then find courage and hope in the final words of Jesus to His disciples that we read in St. Matthew's Gospel:

Now the eleven disciples went to Galilee, to the mountain to which Jesus had directed them.

When they saw him, they worshiped him; but some doubted. And Jesus came and said to them, "All authority in heaven and on earth has been given to me. Go therefore and make disciples of all nations, baptizing them in the name of the Father and of the Son and of the Holy Spirit, and teaching them to obey everything that I have commanded you. And remember, I am with you always, to the end of the age (Mt. 28:16-20).

We notice that some of the disciples doubted. This is not surprising since they have not as yet received the anointing of the Holy Spirit. We too have doubts and are often confused by the many twists and turns that have their origin in Satan, the prince of lies. Let us remember that we have the Holy Spirit just as the disciples did. Their doubts disappeared and they were filled with power as Jesus promised: "But you will receive power when the Holy Spirit has come upon you; and you will be my witnesses in Jerusalem, in all Judea and Samaria, and to the ends of the earth"(Acts 1:8).

These chapters were written to proclaim that the power of the Holy Spirit is still a powerful force in the Church. This is true despite the fact that Satan is still at work trying to destroy the Body of Christ in all of its facets. Here the Gospel is proclaimed in all of its richness and power. We also have many witnesses who have shared their testimonies in areas of personal conversion, forgiveness, healing, and subsequent ministry. This spiritual awakening has empowered them to be credible and effective witnesses in testifying to and spreading the Good News.

I am deeply grateful to all who have been true spiritual friends and helped me on my own conversion journey. I am also very much indebted to all who have worked with me through the years in the ministry of evangelization at home and abroad. A very sincere thank you also goes out to those who have helped me in preparing this manuscript. May it be an instrument of light and hope to all who read it. Many, many blessings to all. Yes, Jesus is still with us.

"Lives of great men all remind us
we can make our lives sublime,
And, departing, leave behind us.
Footprints on the sands of time."
(Henry Wadsworth Longfellow)

ONE

Pilgrimage to Our Father's House

We begin our reflections on God's Word and action in His Church by quoting what is regarded as the most important verse in the Bible: Jesus' response to Thomas: "I am the way, and the truth, and the life. No one comes to the Father except through me." (Jn. 14:6). Our pilgrimage then, to the Father, can only come through Jesus. All claims of religious denominations of direct access to God apart from Jesus are false. We pray that all people will finally come to Jesus as Lord and through Him finally rest in the arms of the Father.

Preparing for the Year of the Father, 2000 AD, St. John Paul II gave us this beautiful prayer to welcome the new millennium:

> God, Creator of Heaven and Earth, Father of Jesus and our Father, blessed are you, Lord, Father in heaven, who, in your infinite mercy, stooped down to us in our distress and gave us Jesus, your Son, born of woman, to be our Savior and friend, our brother and redeemer. We thank you, good Father, for the gift of the Jubilee Year; make it a time of favor for us, the year of a great return to the Father's house,

where, full of love, you await your straying children to embrace them in your forgiveness and welcome them to your table, in their festive garments. We praise you, Father, forever! Father most merciful, during this Holy Year may our love for you and for our neighbor grow ever stronger; may Christ's disciples promote justice and peace; may they proclaim the Good News to the poor; and may the Church our Mother direct her love especially to the little ones and the neglected. We praise you, Father, forever! Father of justice, may the Great Jubilee be the fitting time for all Catholics to rediscover the joy of living by your word and obeying your will; may they know the goodness of fraternal communion, as they break bread together and praise you in hymns and inspired songs. We praise you, Father, forever! Father, rich in mercy, may the holy Jubilee be a time of openness, of dialogue and encounter, among all who believe in Christ and with the followers of other religions: in your immense love, be bountiful in mercy to all. We praise you, Father, forever! O God, Almighty Father, as we make our way to you, our ultimate destiny, may all your children experience the gentle company of Mary most holy, image of purest love, whom you chose to be Mother of Christ and Mother of the Church. We praise you, Father, forever! To you, Father of life, eternal source of all that is, highest good and everlasting light, be honor and glory, praise and thanksgiving, with the Son and with the Spirit, for ages unending. Amen.

Our Holy Father offered us a vision and focus in this Year of God the Father. We were to contemplate our Christian journey as "a pilgrimage to the house of the Father."

We were to reflect on His unconditional love in a special way as it is lavished on the "prodigal son." He reminded us that the progression of the pilgrimage begins in the human heart of each person. It then expands to the believing community and beyond to the whole human family.

The story of the prodigal son (Lk. 15:11-32) is surely one of the most heart-warming and compassionate teachings of Jesus in the Gospels. When we conducted a Reconciliation Service for our children at St. Veronica's Church, we usually placed the image of the father, warmly embracing the sinful son, on the cover of the booklet. I always asked the children to look at the image and allow its message to sink in. They would gaze and gaze in silence, and soon they were absorbed in the scene. This message is at the heart of the Gospel and wonderfully summarizes the most essential goal of Christian life — to find ourselves plunged into the bosom of the Father and find our ultimate rest in His heart.

The yearning of the human heart for the Father's embrace has expressed itself in nefarious ways down through human history. The multiplicity of deities reveals the spiritual longing and hunger that is inherent to the human spirit as it cries out for union with its creator.

Finally, God began to reveal Himself to the Israelites, our fathers in faith. He revealed Himself as a faithful God and entered into a covenant with His children, promising under oath that He would be their God and they would be His people (Lev. 26:12). We see these solemn promises repeated time and time again by God, such as to Abraham, Moses, and David.

In this ongoing revelation, God showed Himself to be a loving, caring provider for His children.

> For the Lord's portion is his people, Jacob his allotted inheritance. In a desert land he found him, in a barren and howling waste. He shielded him and cared for him; he guarded him as the apple of his eye, like an eagle that stirs up its nest and hovers over its young, that spreads its wings to catch them and carries them aloft (Deut 32:9-11).

God reminds his people through Isaiah that the instinct of maternal tenderness is but a reflection of His infinite and eternal parenting:

> Can a woman forget her nursing child, or show no compassion for the child of her womb? Even these may forget, yet I will not forget you. See, I have inscribed you on the palms of my hands; your walls are continually before me (Is 49:15-16).

How intimate, how endearing, and how comforting are these words. How reassuring, how encouraging is His love! In all of these loving revelations in word and action in the Old Testament, our Heavenly Father is preparing the way for the ultimate act of love that would unfold in Jesus. "For God so loved the world that he gave his one and only Son, that whoever believes in him shall not perish but have eternal life" (Jn. 3:16). Jesus came in loving obedience to his Father to reveal the mystery hidden from the ages (Col 1: 26-27). In St. Luke's Gospel, Jesus' first and last words concern his Father. In the Temple he reminds his parents of his mission: "Why were you looking for me? Did you not know that I must be in my Father's house?" (Lk. 2:49). On the cross his final act was one of loving self-surrender that completed his mission on earth: "Father, into your hands I commend my spirit" (Lk. 23:46).

Jesus came as the Good Shepherd who would seek out and find those who were lost and through His cross and resurrection lead them home to the Father. "Everything that the Father gives me will come to me, and I will not reject anyone who comes to me, because I came down from heaven not to do my own will but the will of the one who sent me. And this is the will of the one who sent me, that I should not lose anything of what he gave me, but that I should raise it (on) the last day" (Jn. 6:38-39).

Jesus tells us that only through him can we come to the Father: "I am the way and the truth and the life. No one comes to the Father except through me"(Jn.

14:6). Yet he assures us that no one comes to him unless the Father draws them (Jn. 6:44). Let us meditate on this scene then. Our Father's love, acting like a powerful magnetic force, is drawing us to Himself through Jesus our Risen Savior. The force of love is the Holy Spirit whom our Father desires to give to those who ask.

> What father among you would hand his son a snake when he asks for a fish? Or hand him a scorpion when he asks for an egg? If you then, who are wicked, know how to give good gifts to your children, how much more will the Father in heaven give the Holy Spirit to those who ask him? (Lk. 11:11-13).

Surely this is the most welcome news to us, whose traditional attitude to our Heavenly Father has been one of distance, mistrust, and misplaced fear. How comforting to know that His fatherly heart is yearning to transform us in His love through the Holy Spirit and prepare us for an eternity of bliss in the bosom of the Holy Trinity.

The Year of God the Father was a time of grace to imbibe anew this wonderful message of our Father's love. It is especially urgent that we become witnesses to this love in a culture and a world where fatherless families are on the rise and poor father relationships have had profound negative effects both emotionally and spiritually in the lives of so many. A 2004 study on family life by Cynthia Harper of the University of

Pennsylvania and Sara McLanahan of Princeton examined a group of teenage boys and followed their progress over a fifteen-year period. Of the boys who were living in families headed by mothers, 13% were incarcerated by their early thirties. However, boys with father-headed homes had only a 5% rate. Boys living in stepfather homes increased the odds of being incarcerated by almost threefold. In the men-bashing, father-bashing culture of extreme feminism and other groups that get so much media attention these days, studies such as this one are important. They reinforce what we already know about the importance of a healthy nuclear family. If the place of our human parenting is so important, it is because God our Father designed it so. But don't look to your family TV shows for help in reinforcing the positive values of good fathering.

A study by the National Fatherhood Initiative (NFI) points out that only 15 prime-time shows — or 15% of the 102 available on the networks — have fathers as central characters. This is rightly a cause for concern since 25 million children are growing up without their biological fathers in the home. The NFI study shows that not only are fathers mostly absent in prime-time programming, when they do appear, they are third-rate caliber. NFI concludes that only four of the fifteen shows with fathers are positive characterizations, that is, they are involved with their children, offer moral support, are competent as fathers and make the family their priority. It is also interesting to note that no prime-time shows on Saturday night had a father figure, even though that was the most likely time that the whole family would watch TV together.

Where human parenting is anointed and blessed by God it will reflect His perfect, eternal parenting. It becomes our Father's love incarnate and provides a grace-filled steppingstone for the child to enter into an intimate spiritual journey in the arms of God our Father. Other research bears this out. If both parents go to Church regularly, 79% of their children remain faithful to God. If only the Mom goes, 15% tend to keep the faith. But if only the Dad attends, the percentage rises dramatically to 50%. What a difference a good father makes.

The story of St. Thérèse of Lisieux brings us a wonderful example of a saintly, loving father's role in leading his beloved daughters on a pilgrimage of profound spiritual intimacy with their Heavenly Father. In her unique and splendid simplicity, St. Thérèse would describe her prayer as closing her eyes, picturing herself climbing up on God the Father's lap, cuddling up and falling asleep in His arms. Here in brilliant imagery is presented to us a spiritual journey that scaled heights reached only by the few. Her Mom died when Therese was just a little girl. However, her father lavished the most tender love to all his daughters and especially to little Therese. He named her "his *petite reine*, little queen, to whom all treasures belonged." His faith, piety, tenderness, caring, and direction paved the way for his daughters to enter a deep and intimate relationship with their Heavenly Father. Here is an example of an insecure child in need of a loving father:

As I was timid and sensitive by nature, I did not know how to defend myself and was content to cry without saying a word and without complaining *even to you* (her eldest sister) what I was suffering. I didn't have enough virtue, however, to rise above these miseries of life, and so my poor little heart suffered very much. Every evening I was back at home, fortunately, and then my heart expanded. I would jump up on Papa's lap telling about the marks they had given me, and his kiss made me forget my troubles (*Story of a Soul*, 53).

What we learn from this exchange is that Therese's unconditional trust in her loving Papa was formed through the years due to his immense and unconditional love. Papa's ability to love as he did was itself formed and perfected by the Abba love flowing from within him through the Holy Spirit, transforming him interiorly through Word and Sacrament, and the rich spiritual communion he and his beloved wife had passed on. Here is a glimpse of the spiritual life that they lived as a family:

There reigned in the Martin family a solid faith that saw God in life's events, paying Him a permanent homage: family prayers together, morning attendance at Mass, frequent reception of Holy Communion — rare in an epoch when

Jansenism continued its ravages — Sunday Vespers, retreats. Their whole life revolved around the liturgical year, pilgrimages, a scrupulous regard for fasts and abstinences. There was nothing stiff and bigoted in this family...They could be active and contemplative, feeding abandoned children, tramps and the aged..." (*Story of a Soul,* 4).

What a wonderful example of what a Catholic home can be; how inspiring; how encouraging.

On Pentecost Sunday 2008, Pope Benedict XVI proclaimed:

Today I would like to extend this invitation to everyone: Let us rediscover, dear brothers and sisters, the beauty of being baptized in the Holy Spirit; let us be aware again of our baptism and our confirmation, sources of grace that are always present. Let us ask the Virgin Mary to obtain a renewed Pentecost for the Church again today, a Pentecost that will spread in everyone the joy of living and witnessing to the Gospel.

He also noted that the Acts of the Apostles presents the outpouring of the Holy Spirit at Pentecost as the "crowning moment of Jesus' mission" and the fulfillment of John the Baptist's prophecy: "He who comes after me...will baptize you in the Holy Spirit" (Mt 3:11).

> In effect Jesus' whole mission was aimed at giving the Spirit of God to men and baptizing them in the bath of regeneration. This was realized through his glorification (John 7:39), that is through his death and resurrection: Then the Spirit of God was poured out in a superabundant way, like a waterfall able to purify every heart, to extinguish the flames of evil and ignite the fire of divine love in the world (Pope Benedict).

As we continue our pilgrimage to our Father, let us pray for the anointing of the Holy Spirit to be the Fire and Light that unites us as family and reveals all the more intensely and clearly our Father's paternal love drawing us through Jesus to Himself. Let the Martin Family be with us on our journey.

TWO

Awakening to Our Father's Love in the Power of the Holy Spirit

Here we begin with the fuller quote and context that surrounds John 14:6:

"Do not let your hearts be troubled. Believe in God, believe also in me. In my Father's house there are many dwelling places. If it were not so, would I have told you that I go to prepare a place for you? And if I go and prepare a place for you, I will come again and will take you to myself, so that where I am, there you may be also. And you know the way to the place where I am going." Thomas said to him, "Lord, we do not know where you are going. How can we know the way?" Jesus said to him, "I am the way, and the truth, and the life. No one comes to the Father except through me. If you know me, you will know my Father also. From now on you do know him and have seen him." Philip said to him, "Lord, show us the Father, and we will be satisfied." Jesus said to him, "Have I been with you all this time, Philip, and you still do not know me? Whoever has seen me has seen the Father. How can you say, 'Show us the Father'?"

In my message for Christmas 2016 to my family and friends, I addressed the issue of fatherlessness and the deep pain of loss that causes so many a depth of emptiness. Trying in vain to resolve that pain with what the world offers only deepens the sense of loss and intensifies frustration until we finally, if fortunate, are led into the arms of our Father, Abba, through the Holy Spirit, and soak in His loving mercy, forgiveness and healing, and ultimately rest in His arms forever in Heaven.

I share that Christmas message here:

The Holy Season of Advent provides us with a wonderful opportunity to enter more deeply into the wonder of the life and love of the Holy Trinity. For surely that was why Jesus chose to share our human nature through the immaculate womb of the Blessed Virgin Mary. He tells us why: "I came that you may have life and have it abundantly" (Jn. 10:10). Jesus clearly reveals to us that he is the only way to this abundant life, in what is regarded as the most important verse in the whole Bible: "I am the way and the truth and the life. No one comes to the Father except through me" (Jn. 14:6). Jesus has made this coming to the Father possible through his passion, death, and glorious resurrection. However, it is the Holy Spirit, coming from the heart of Christ after his ascension, who now reveals the Father and Son glorified. St. Paul makes this revelation clear for us: For those who are led by the Spirit of God are children of God. For you did not receive a spirit of slavery falling back into fear, but a spirit of

adoption, through which we cry, Abba, "Father!"
(Rom. 8:14,15). What a wonderful way to describe
God our Father! *Abba* is a child's intimate address
in Hebrew and Aramaic, such as *Daddy* in our
culture. Likewise, St. Paul asserts: "No one can say,
'Jesus is Lord,' except by the Holy Spirit" (1 Cor.
12:3). To "say" here means "proclaiming from
heart-felt experience." With St. Paul we are all
called to discover the power and riches of our
Baptismal adoption, so that, with him, we can
profess with profound conviction: "I no longer live,
but Christ lives in me" (Gal. 2:20).

Our personal spiritual journey then is
ultimately finding our home in the arms of God our
Father. In God's plan, human fatherhood was
designed to reflect our Heavenly Father's love,
care, guidance, and protection. However, original
sin intervened in a drastic way. St. John Paul II
said, "Original sin attempts to abolish fatherhood...
placing in doubt the truth about God who is Love
and leaving man only with a sense of the master-
slave relationship." Sadly we see more and more
today the condition of absent or broken faith in the
lives of the fatherless. For some, this absence comes
through tragedies such as death; divorce;
abandonment; abuse; and detachment which can be
spiritual, emotional, or physical. Thus *the child
within* is left grieving and impoverished.

Dr. Paul Vitz, former head of the Psychology
Department at the University of New York and a
Catholic convert, did a study of some of the well-

known atheists and found that the common thread among them all was that they had no fathers, basically falling into the list mentioned above. His book, *Faith of the Fatherless,* is indeed a powerful testimony to the great need for faith-filled, loving and caring fathers who will be there with their wives to nurture the faith of their children. Today, our prisons are filled with fatherless convicts, and gang members who fall into the same category roam the streets of our cities.

Over the years we have encountered this father-absence in so many of its forms and the heartbreak that it left behind. Our ministry was focused on leading such persons to forgiveness and opening their wounded hearts to Christ, who will breathe in the life-giving, healing love of the Holy Spirit. We also invite our Blessed Mother and St. Joseph to join in this prayer so that painful family memories may be healed.

During Advent, John the Baptist is introduced, as prophesied (Mal. 4:6):"And he shall go before him (Christ) in the spirit and power of Elijah, to turn the hearts of the fathers to the children, and the disobedient to the wisdom of the just; to make ready a people prepared for the Lord" (Lk. 1:17).

Let the Seasons of Advent and Christmas then lead to deeper personal and family renewal, as the Holy Spirit leads us more intimately into the Family of the Holy Trinity. This fulfills the reason for Christ's coming.

God, as Father, is mentioned just eight times in the Old Testament. However, it is in the New Testament that His name appears 166 times.

Through the grace of the Holy Spirit our Father's love is passed on to us in the Church. Parents are blessed with that love in the natural and supernatural levels.

Here I share an experience of that love in a mother tenderly ministering to her unconscious son:

When I went to pray with Michael in the hospital, he was in a coma. All through the time of my visit his Mom was caressing him, stroking his hair, massaging his hands and feet, speaking loving and encouraging words to him. There was no response from Michael, yet Mom did not cease her loving attention. I was very moved by this outpouring of love. What was even more remarkable was that this mother did not see herself as remarkable: She was simply doing what her maternal instinct called her to do. Pouring out her maternal love, even when there was no recognition or response, was totally natural to her; totally ordinary. What a reflection of divine love, I thought, is the love of a mother. When I visited Michael at his home a year later nothing had changed: the maternal love continued to flow without any discernible response.

Preparing to celebrate Pentecost in the Year of God the Father, we were called to again reflect on the central role of the Holy Spirit, as He was revealed to us. As we enter into the Easter Season, the Liturgy of the Word brings us in touch with the exalted teachings of Jesus in St. John's Gospel and the lived experience of Pentecost in the early days of the Church through the Acts of the Apostles. There are some striking contrasts in the pictures painted for us in these readings.

First, we see the clarity of Jesus' teaching about the Father's plan. For St. John, Jesus is the profound preacher who is ever in intimate communion with the Father. It is Jesus, in His own person, who reveals the Father to us. It is through Jesus alone that we come into our Father's arms: Thomas said to him, "Lord, we don't know where you are going, so how can we know the way?" Jesus answered, "I am the way and the truth and the life. No one comes to the Father except through me. If you really know me, you will know my Father as well. From now on, you do know him and have seen him" (Jn. 14: 6, 7). Scholars tell us that the theology of St. John is beautifully summarized in a passage in St. Matthew's Gospel:

> At that time Jesus said, "I thank you, Father, Lord of heaven and earth, because you have hidden these things from the wise and the intelligent and have revealed them to infants; yes, Father, for such was your gracious will. All things have been handed over to me by my Father; and no one knows the Son except the Father, and no one knows the Father except the Son and anyone to whom the Son chooses to reveal him" (Mt. 11:25-27).

Jesus reveals to us His intimacy with the Father and promises that we will share in this very intimacy. In chapter 14, St. John opens up to us what is truly one of the most profound discourses in Scripture leading us into the very heart of the Holy Trinity. The awesome truth is:

Where Jesus abides in the heart of His Father, He is preparing a place for us.

In contrast to the clarity of this teaching of Jesus we find that the disciples do not get it. They are just as dull and obtuse as Jesus' enemies. Like Michael, they are unable to make the connection with and respond to the parenting love of our Father. Yet John uses their ignorance, as expressed in Thomas' question (v. 5), to call forth one of Jesus' most powerful statements that in effect provided the cornerstone of the entire Gospel:

"Jesus said to him, 'I am the way, and the truth, and the life. No one comes to the Father except through me'" (v. 6).

In the Gospel then the contrast that reveals the disciples' ignorance and lack of understanding has a twofold purpose:

1. It allows Jesus the opportunity to expound with clarity the profound truths of the Gospel.

2. It underscores a fundamental theological truth: No one can grasp the mysteries of salvation without the light of the Holy Spirit. So Jesus makes a promise:

> And I will ask the Father, and he will give you another Advocate, to be with you forever. This is the Spirit of truth, whom the world cannot receive, because it neither sees him nor knows him. You know him, because he abides with you, and he will be in you (Jn. 14: 16-17).

This leads us to the other contrast highlighted in the Easter Readings through the Acts of the Apostles: the extraordinary transformation and empowerment brought about in the disciples through the experience of Pentecost. They are now forthright and courageous witnesses of the Resurrection of Jesus, calling their hearers to repentance and Baptism. They have a full grasp of the teachings of Jesus and the import of His Paschal journey that completely evaded them before the anointing of the Holy Spirit.

It is important to note here that to be full witnesses to the Resurrection, the disciples had to visually encounter Christ first. However, this encounter was incomplete until Christ began to live in their hearts at Pentecost. St. Paul expresses the experience of Christ's indwelling in his proclamation:

> I have been crucified with Christ; and it is no longer I who live, but it is Christ who lives in me. And the life I now live in the flesh I live by faith in the Son of God, who loved me and gave himself for me (Gal 2:19-20).

Today, the Church continues the work of the Apostles, giving witness to the Risen Christ primarily through lives transformed in the Holy Spirit and empowered with all the charismatic gifts that Jesus bestowed on His Church for the building up of His Body. We are always inspired and encouraged by the glowing witness of those whose lives have been radically changed and are now called into the ministry of evangelization. We can see in their lives the very presence of the Holy Trinity, and we are encouraged and moved to deeper conversion by their powerful testimony. This has been the blessed experience of Baptism in the Holy Spirit in our day.

In his book *Call to Holiness*, Archbishop Paul Josef Cordes, Episcopal Advisor to the International Catholic Charismatic Renewal Office in Rome, gives us an in-depth overview of renewal in the Church today:

> The experience of 'Baptism in the Holy Spirit' is the certain and sometimes overwhelming "realization" of the loving nearness of God proclaimed in the Church's message and encountered in the individual act of faith. It is a threshold of spiritual life that is crossed, bringing trust in the Father and a desire to being open to the teaching of the Holy Spirit. It constantly deepens our faith, so confirming our "conviction about things we do not see" (Heb 11:1) and making possible the perception of God's effective presence. This experiential perception reveals God in His immense incomprehensibility as well as in His loving and Fatherly care (12).

In a world today that has lost sight of God and is wallowing in the mud of confusion and despair, there is an urgent cry for witnesses who proclaim with joy the reality of our Father's love being poured out through Jesus in the Holy Spirit. In his address to the Renewal Gathering in Rome, Pope John Paul II had this to say:

> Today the Church rejoices at the renewed confirmation of the prophet Joel's words: "I will

pour my Spirit upon all flesh" (Acts 2:17). You, present here, are the tangible proof of this "outpouring" of the Spirit. Each movement is different from the others, but they all are united in the same communion and for the same mission...

Today, I cry out to all of you gathered here in St. Peter's Square and to all Christians: Open yourselves docilely to the gifts of the Spirit! Accept gratefully and obediently the charisms which the Spirit never ceases to bestow on us! Do not forget that every charism is given for the common good, that is for the whole Church.

There is a hunger in every human soul for the loving embrace of our Heavenly Father. Yet, as with the disciples, that embrace has so many obstacles. So often in ministry I have witnessed the inner spiritual and emotional aching that has been described in terms of darkness, great emptiness, and a gnawing sense of loss. I will invite them to open their hearts to Christ and surrender to his loving embrace. I ask Jesus to breathe the Holy Spirit into their hearts so that they can experience the love of God our Father drawing them to Himself. Often there is struggle, disbelief that God loves them, fear that this exercise will fail, and the end result will be worse than the first, an exaggerated sense of unworthiness, a sense of condemnation, and deep mistrust. Yet as we open ourselves to the gentle love of Christ and the anointing of the Holy Spirit, light begins to flood the darkness. Fear begins to dissipate. Chains of hurt and anger begin to crumble. A sense of freedom and liberation begins to replace slavish torment. A sense of family replaces the feeling of abandonment. And above all, a sense of wholesomeness replaces that of sin.

Having awakened to this redeeming and healing love, perhaps for the first time Jesus' proclamation about His mission rings true, "The Spirit of the Lord is upon me, because he has anointed me to bring good news to the poor. He has sent me to proclaim release to the captives and recovery of sight to the blind, to let the oppressed go free, to proclaim the year of the Lord's favor" (Lk. 4: 18-19). What a blessing to know that the Gospel is for real. It works! As we continue to experience our Father's eternal parenting love, let us become witnesses to those who, like Michael, are still unaware of the flood of love that surrounds them.

THREE

The Riches of Baptism

Each year, the celebration of the Feast of Pentecost invites us to continue our reflection on the central role the Holy Spirit plays in the life and growth of the Church and in our individual spiritual walk. Let's explore some spiritual and psychological parallels in an effort to highlight the fundamental role our baptismal gifts play in our spiritual health and growth.

Today, as the Church is experiencing a new outpouring of the Holy Spirit, we are witnessing conversions that are life-changing and radically redirecting people in life journeys and ministries that they would never have previously envisioned. This life changing experience begins with Baptism in the Holy Spirit.

This spiritual phenomenon has touched the hearts of over two hundred million Catholics, and counting, since 1967. There's a common thread: It begins with an experience of unconditional love flowing from our Heavenly Father.

Briefly, here is the story of Father Philip Mulryne, a star soccer player in the English League, who took a break from the game after thirteen years, and returned to his native Belfast for a rest. Here he was introduced by his sister to spiritual literature, and a Charismatic Prayer Group, where he was baptized in the Holy Spirit. From this experience and his participating in the Legion of Mary, he felt the call to priesthood. Today he is a Dominican priest spreading the Word of God to young and old alike.

We see, that in this experience we discover the awesome truth of what it means to be baptized into Christ.

When we speak to some people who have not experienced the Baptism in the Holy Spirit, they say that they have already received the Holy Spirit in Baptism, Confirmation and – as the case may be – Ordination. We respond, as Cardinal Suenens did with a question: "You undoubtedly have the Holy Spirit, but does the Holy Spirit have you?"

It is very possible to have received all the sacraments and to be a practical atheist at the same time. The sacramental gifts will lay dormant until they are activated by an act of self-surrender to the Lordship of Jesus, who in turn will release the Holy Spirit's gifts within us.

For the first time, many are realizing that God loves them with a most tender and steadfast love. They are now coming to know, in a warm and personal way, the God who to this point was distant and impersonal—the deity they only knew about. This is the starting point for a lifelong journey of spiritual growth. The experience of divine love opens the human soul as a sunflower responds to the warmth and light of the sun. We can therefore say without hesitation that the degree to which we experience our Baptismal anointing will determine the quality and health of our entire spiritual journey. Let me explain by giving a parallel in our psychological development.

In the course of studies in psychology, we had to do a book report on Erik Erikson's classic, *Identity and the Life*

Cycle. In this book, Erikson charts eight stages of personality development that are interconnected and follow the epigenetic principle. He explains: "Somehow generalized, this principle states that anything that grows has a ground plan, and that out of this ground plan the parts arise, each part having its time of special ascendancy, until all parts have arisen to form a functioning whole" (53).

The development of personality in the extra-uterine stage begins with a sense of basic trust. This sense grows out of the parents' (primarily the mother's) day-to-day nurturing in all its facets. It is in this environment of unconditional love that the child develops a sense of self-worth. If the primitive thinking of the infant were to be verbalized, it would go something like this: "I am good and I am lovable because I am loved." Basic trust then becomes the bedrock of all personality development.

It is this sense of well-being that moves the infant to the next stage, autonomy, which develops in sync with the sphincter muscles. Control over bowel and bladder brings a new sense of well-being to the infant that begins the journey of mastering one's environment. It is this crucial development during the "terrible twos" that will in turn pave the way for the next stage which is initiative. At age four to five, children begin to assert their power and control over the world through directing play and other social interaction. Thus the process continues, stage building upon stage, till the final stage of integrity is reached in adult maturity.

When there is neglect and/or abuse in the first year of life – despite the most loving care and attention in the years that follow – the results can be devastating. In a recent TV documentary of sisters adopted after abuse and neglect in infancy, the tragic tale of pain and heartbreak was graphically told. We saw the years of heroic efforts, of loving adoptive parents, rendered void by children who seemed to have been set on a course of self-destruction.

No matter how much love and attention these wonderful parents showered on them, the results were always the same. These children would not accept their love. They could not. The damage of abuse and neglect in that first year of life left an indelible impression on those children's psyches. They felt unlovable and unworthy. No matter how heroic and unconditional the love, attention, and self-sacrifice of their adoptive parents, these children could not change that deeply imbedded negative sense of self. One of the sisters became a prostitute while the other finally settled down to some form of a normal life.

It is interesting that St. Paul uses the term adoption to describe what happens in Baptism. As an infant is personally chosen by a loving family to share all the blessings and privileges of a happy home, so in Baptism we are adopted into the Family of the Holy Trinity to share the perfect, intimate love and communion of Father, Son and Holy Spirit.

> Those who are led by the Spirit of God are children of God. For you did not receive a spirit of slavery to fall back into fear, but you received a spirit of adoption, through which we cry, "Abba, Father!" The Spirit itself bears witness with our spirit that we are children of God, and if children,

then heirs, heirs of God and joint heirs with Christ (Rom. 8:14-17).

Paul, who wrote in Greek, introduces us to the word "Abba" which comes from Hebrew and Aramaic. It is baby talk for "Daddy". This word appears only three times in the Bible.

We had a wonderful experience of the pathos of this word during a pilgrimage to the Holy Land some years ago. Our group was gathering in our hotel lobby in Jerusalem preparing for an evening event. Right in front of us was seated a young Israeli family with their two little boys playing on the carpet. After a while the little one, aged about three, tripped over his older brother and fell. Then he picked himself up and ran right into his dad's arms crying, "Abba, Abba." His father picked him up and hugged him. He was healed immediately. We were very touched by this encounter as we saw firsthand the powerful meaning which the word "Abba" carries. Somehow, we sensed that this was one of the very special blessings of the pilgrimage for us, recalling our own experience of Abba's love when we encountered the riches of Baptism.

In the healing ministry we have witnessed the loving power of God touch deep-seated wounds of early childhood abuse and neglect. In what we call the healing of memories, the Lord in His love can go back in life to these wounds that are deeply buried in the unconscious and heal them. Only divine love can do this.

After one such healing experience, I received this note:

After all my years in professional counseling, I've never felt the peace or total renewal as I felt when I left your office. Since I've seen you my attitude has completely changed, and I feel that the overbearing feelings of depression, anxiety and guilt are all but gone.

What this person experienced was the unconditional love of God the Father in the power of the Holy Spirit. The warmth of healing light and love now filled the dark hole of depression, left by rejection and neglect in infancy.

What does all this have to do with spiritual growth? The epigenetic principle that governs biological and psychological development can equally be applied here. We can conclude: Growth in the spiritual life has its foundation in the experience of Our Father's unconditional love. It is this experience of divine love that sets the stage for childlike trust in God. Trust is therefore the fruit of a constant and steadfast love. Trust in God is the result of a loving encounter with God, our Father, through Jesus in the power and presence of the Holy Spirit.

In his wonderful book on St. Therese of Lisieux, Father Bernard Bro, O.P. speaks of the roots of her spiritual journey:

She had discovered the true face of the God of Jesus, offering himself to us in weakness and, like a beggar, waiting for our trust. And she knew that the time for total trust had come. Never to achieve anything worthwhile again, but only to accept being exceeded – forever – by the excess of love confronting her. Then for her, as for the Good Thief, as for St. Peter, as for the Samaritan woman, as for all the poor and sinful, the impossible step became possible: trust, making what in the end seemed too far away suddenly within reach (*The Little Way*, 43).

We have discovered in our day once again that this grace of encountering "the excess of love" comes to us through the Holy Spirit. This gift is given at Baptism and somehow, somewhere, in our spiritual journey it needs to be unlocked if we are to begin an intimate walk with God. Should this not happen we will spend a life in spiritual struggle, never getting to first base. As with the adopted sisters, a dark hole of spiritual emptiness will persist despite personal efforts to live a virtuous life.

The Good News is that God our Father wants each one of us to receive His overflowing life and love in the person of the Holy Spirit. Jesus assures us of this: "If you then, who are evil, know how to give good gifts to your children, how much more will the heavenly Father give the Holy Spirit to those who ask him!" (Lk. 11:12).

The first stage in spiritual growth is the infusion of sanctifying grace at the moment of Baptism that gives us a new life and a new nature. By one awesome touch of God we are transformed internally and become sharers in the Divine Nature. Speaking of this extraordinary mystery, St. Gregory of Nazianzus declares:

Baptism is God's most beautiful and magnificent gift...We call it gift, grace, anointing, enlightenment, garment of immortality, bath of rebirth, seal, and most precious gift. It is called gift because it is conferred on those who bring nothing of their own; grace since it is given even to the guilty; Baptism because sin is buried in the water; anointing for it is priestly and royal as are those who are anointed; enlightenment because it radiates light; clothing since it veils our shame; bath because it washes; and seal as it is our guard and the sign of God's lordship. (c.f. Catechism, 1213ff).

To see the Sacrament of Baptism in terms of a loving encounter with the Holy Trinity, we might describe it thus: God our Father calls us by name to come to Him. Through the arms of Jesus, He reaches out and draws us to Himself. Through the anointing of the Holy Spirit He breathes a new life into us that intimately unites us to the Godhead. It is through the Holy Spirit that our Father speaks those words of paternal affection that He addressed to His Son at the Baptism at the Jordan: "You are my child, my beloved; with you I am well pleased" (c.f. Mk. 1:11). Jesus draws us close to His Sacred Heart and unites us in intimate love with all the baptized who persevere in grace. He prepares a place at His table for us and guarantees a permanent place in His heavenly home. (Jn. 14:2).

For those who have been baptized in the Holy Spirit, this newfound intimacy with God has led to some wonderful discoveries.

Here we include a letter I received from a high school student who had attended a Retreat with her high school graduating class in the fall of 1978.

Father, I hope you are feeling rested by now from the Retreat. I am still a little tired, but otherwise I am feeling great inside. I just wanted to let you know that the Retreat in Kirkridge has been the best experience of my life. I found out that the Father is present in my life and I feel so comfortable with Him now. I discovered that my class really does care for me and love me. Also, I found that I've been blessed to have someone like you, Father, who have led me to encounter the face of Jesus. When we were ready to leave on Wednesday morning and Father Chuck asked if anyone had anything to say to you before we left, there was silence. How could anyone have said in a sentence or two what we encountered in that Retreat? So, our faces and eyes told you all that had to be said.

Thank you for opening my eyes to someone's love, God's, that I have been ignoring for some time. You have helped me to find out who He is, who my classmates are, and who I am. I know that the Retreat will only be a beautiful memory if I do not work on it. But I also believe that with some effort the Retreat could last forever. Thanks for giving me this wonderful start.

As I am writing this letter to you, I can feel Jesus' warm presence in my heart. He is helping me express what I feel. You know that I am not capable of writing down all the beautiful feelings I have inside myself right now. For one thing, I'd probably be here infinitely trying to express the wonders I've found from the Father's presence. Thanks to you, Father. I believe that I am on my way to achieving total inner peace, for I am experiencing glimpses of it right now, and it is so great that I cannot put it into words. I want to share my letter to God with you:

Dear God, my Retreat has really stirred my inner being. My faith has been aroused more than it ever has been. Right now, my heart feels so warmed by your presence and love. It is a feeling I never want to leave me. I wonder why my life could not have been this beautiful before... Right now, as I am writing this letter, I feel I am talking right to my heart because I know that is just where you are. I don't have to look to the sky to wonder whether you are there and listening, because I know that you are right here, in my own body, in my heart.

Always before, my faith had seen you as some superior force that governs the destiny of men's lives. I always, or almost always, pictured you as looking upon us, but not in us, or in me. But now I have discovered that you are in me. Lord, do not ever leave me because without you I am nothing.

Even when I first came to this Retreat I was hesitant in wanting to pray and learn more about you. I am now overjoyed at the thought that I want to pray and learn more about you, now that you have entered my heart. I want to begin to discover the mysteries that still lie between us so that I can become closer to you.

Father, how great you must be. You have gifted me with precious things. How great you must be to have created someone like our priest. I believe that because of his affection and warm-heartedness I have come to know you. If I feel he is so great, how much greater must you be. How much more could you make me feel loved and special. So I want to thank you, Lord, for my class that I have come to know and love with great affection. They showed me that they also care about me. I want to thank you for Father. I believe without him my faith would have never given me that chance to love you the way I do now. He made me realize that I could have good times and have a strong faith at the same time. Lord, I love you especially more when I think of your goodness and unselfishness to give me a chance to love Father for the gift that he is to us all.

I find it hard to believe how much my faith has grown since the Retreat. It's almost unbelievable how much closer I feel to you. Never in my life have I felt so near you. By my faith in you, Lord, I have grown closer to my class. Thanks for our priests, teachers and staff who have helped complete the feeling that I am experiencing now. Thanks, Father Abba — *Helen*

What a beautiful testimony! Here we see the action of the Holy Spirit, so present and active in spirit, soul, and body, and so beautifully expressed in the lived experience of a teenage young woman. What a wonderful way to prepare for adulthood! During my four years at St. Thomas

Aquinas High School, we conducted over forty overnight Retreats with the students. It was indeed a great blessing to experience our students' joy as they discovered, through the Holy Spirit, the hidden riches of their Baptism and Confirmation.

Through the Holy Spirit, there is a wholesome sense of belonging to God and rejoicing in this belonging. There is a unity with and loyalty to the Church. There is a deep desire to grow in holiness and a longing to share this experience with others. In our experiences with evangelization, over 90% of those attending the Schools of Evangelization were already baptized in the Holy Spirit. Their lively faith and ardent love of God enrich all our parish ministries.

Discovery of our Father's unconditional love through the Holy Spirit in Baptism sets the stage for discovering the power of God's love in the other Sacraments. Many have told me that they now have been drawn to a deeper love of Christ in the Eucharist. They are now discovering the consolation of his mercy in Reconciliation. Renewed couples witness to a healing and deepening of their love in the Sacrament of Matrimony. Priests have been empowered tremendously in their life and ministry. I am certain that vocations to priesthood and religious life will flourish when we introduce our young people to the anointing of the Holy Spirit. I believe that many vocations that are on the rocks will be healed and renewed when they discover the joy and consolation of their Baptism.

Finally, the story of a kitten born in the wild can mirror the struggle of Christians who have not discovered our Father's loving touch. One morning in early July

(2010), we found two little kittens at our back door. They were hungry but when approached they would run into the bushes. So we would place the food on a dish and leave. All of the Rectory staff loved them right away and yearned to hold and stroke them but to no avail. This went on for about a month until finally they allowed the first human touch. There was rejoicing in the Rectory. We named them Hansel and Gretel. Unfortunately Gretel died in an accident. Hansel remained to experience the rich rewards of human touch. In the same way, our Father waits for our surrender to His paternal embrace. When we do, there is rejoicing in Heaven and our lives will never be the same again after we find the excess of love in our Abba's arms.

FOUR

The Gift of the Holy Spirit:
Transforming and Empowering

We go to some of the great sainted theologians of the early Church to teach us about the Holy Spirit and how he functions in the life and work of the Holy Trinity.

Baptism gives us the grace of new birth in God the Father, through his Son, in the Holy Spirit. For those who bear God's Spirit are led to the Word, that is to the Son, and the Son presents them to the Father, and the Father confers incorruptibility on them. And it is impossible to see God's Son without the Spirit, and no one can approach the Father without the Son, for the knowledge of the Father is the Son, and the knowledge of God's Son is obtained through the Holy Spirit. — St. Irenaeus

The Old Testament proclaimed the Father clearly, but the Son more obscurely. The New Testament revealed the Son and gave us a glimpse of the divinity of the Spirit. Now the Spirit dwells among us and grants us a clearer vision of himself. It was not prudent, when the divinity of the Father had not yet been confessed, to proclaim the Son openly and, when the divinity of the Son was not yet admitted, to add the Holy Spirit as an extra burden, to speak somewhat daringly...By advancing and progressing 'from glory to glory,' the light of the Trinity will shine in ever more brilliant ways. — St. Gregory of Nazianzus

The *Catechism of the Catholic Church* (CCC) teaches us about the role of the Holy Spirit:

The Church, a communion living in the faith of the Apostles which she transmits, is the place we know the Holy Spirit: –in the Scriptures he inspired; –in the Tradition, to which the Church Fathers are always timely witnesses; –in the Magisterium, which he assists; –in the sacramental liturgy, through the words and symbols, in which the Holy Spirit puts us into communion with Christ; –in prayer, wherein he intercedes for us; –in charisms and ministries by which the Church is built up; –in the signs of apostolic and missionary life; –in the witness of saints through whom he manifests his holiness and continues the work of salvation.

The Joint Mission of the Son and the Spirit:
The One whom the Father sent into our hearts, the Spirit of his Son, is truly God (Gal. 4:6). Consubstantial with the Father and the Son, the Spirit is inseparable from them, in both the inner

life of the Trinity and his gift of love for the world. In adoring the Holy Trinity, life giving, consubstantial, and indivisible, the Church's faith also professes the distinction of persons. When the Father sends his Word, he always sends his Breath. In their mission, the Son and the Holy Spirit are distinct but inseparable. To be sure, it is Christ who is seen, the visible image of the invisible God, but it is the Spirit who reveals him."

Jesus is Christ, "anointed," because the Spirit is his anointing, and everything that occurs from the Incarnation on derives from this fullness (cf. Jn 3:34). When Christ is finally glorified (Jn 7:39), he can in turn send the Spirit from his place with the Father to those who believe in him: he communicates to them his glory (cf Jn. 17:22), that is the Holy Spirit who glorifies him (cf Jn. 16:14). From that time on, this joint mission will be manifested in the children adopted by the Father in the Body of his Son: the mission of the Spirit of adoption is to unite them to Christ and make them live in him. (688-690).

The feast of Pentecost calls us to meditate on the extraordinary mystery of salvation as the Holy Spirit unfolds it in the Church's ongoing celebration of the Paschal Mystery. We become aware that it is the Holy Spirit who unveils this mystery for us and opens us to the overflowing life of the Holy Trinity that brings about a radical transformation in our lives.

This radical transformation is reflected in St. John's Gospel at the wedding feast at Cana. This first of the "signs" (Jn. 2:11) demonstrates the abundance of life in the messianic age and the transforming power of grace that makes us a new creation. St. John asserts in the following words of Jesus that it is the Holy Spirit who gives us the experience of this abundant life: "If anyone thirsts, let him come to me, let him drink who believes in me. Scripture has it: `From within him rivers of living water shall flow.' (Here he was referring to the Spirit, whom those who came to believe in him were to receive.)" (Jn. 7:37-39). This radical change bringing overflowing life was the experience of Pentecost and the ongoing experience of the early Church. The story of St. Paul's conversion experience is another wonderful example of how radical and awesome this transformation is when we are renewed in Christ through the power of the Holy Spirit. Paul saw himself as a new creation, completely refashioned in the person of Christ and fired up by the Spirit.

One of the first gifts of the Holy Spirit is the experience of intimacy with the Holy Trinity. St. Paul proclaims this reality in his famous words: "I have been crucified with Christ and the life I live now is not my own; Christ is living in me" (Gal. 2:19-20). St. Paul also tells us (Gal. 4:6) that it is the Holy Spirit who reveals our Father in heaven as a loving "Abba", which is the Aramaic equivalent of "Daddy". The intimacy that Jesus shared with his Father, he now shares with his Church through the Holy Spirit. "As the Father has loved me, so I have loved you. Live on in my love" (Jn. 15:9).

Today a similar spiritual elation grips those who experience Baptism in the Holy Spirit. Listen, once again, to Father Michael Scanlon, T.O.R., former President of the Franciscan University of Steubenville, describe his experience:

> I immediately knelt down in the middle of the discussion group and said, "I want to be baptized in the Holy Spirit." ... The Spirit fell. It was primarily an experience of prayer, but prayer unlike any other I had experienced or studied. I was lost in God, one with the fullness of life. I wanted nothing more than to know God the way I knew him at that moment, intimately united to him. I let myself go in praise and prayer. God was all I had. He was all I wanted. He was all I needed. I knelt there for many minutes until I was asked to move so that the discussion could proceed. I sat in the corner and God immersed me in fire (*Let the Fire Fall*, 81).

Meet Sr. Briege McKenna, O.S.C. Crippling rheumatoid arthritis threatened to leave her in a wheelchair for the remainder of her life. While at a retreat in 1970, she relates,

> The only prayer I said was, "Jesus, please help me." At that moment I felt a hand touch my head and thought it was the priest who had come over to me. I opened my eyes and no one was there, but there was a power going through my body. It's difficult to describe the feeling, but I often describe it this way: it's like a banana being peeled.

I looked down. My fingers had been stiff but not deformed like my feet. There had been sores on my elbows. I looked at myself. My fingers were limber, the sores were gone, and I could see that my feet, in sandals were no longer deformed...That was a miraculous healing, but my inner life saw the greatest change. Through the charismatic renewal, I experienced the release of the Holy Spirit. I have a new vision of the Church, as though I was seeing the Eucharist and the Sacrament of Reconciliation through new glasses. I was seeing more clearly God's great love for us and what he has given us. (*Miracles Do Happen*).

My personal experience was in Atlantic City at a Charismatic Conference in the mid-seventies. We gathered for a priests' day on Monday after the weekend experience. The hall was full of priests and the presentations were very inspiring. However, as we prepared for Mass the entire gathering entered into the prayer of praise with a power and force that I had never experienced before. I was overwhelmed by the love of God. Though I am not an emotional person and pride myself in keeping my feelings under control, I was overcome with a feeling of love. Tears began to flow so profusely that my shirt was wet as if by perspiration. Perhaps for the first time I knew that God, my Father, loved me unconditionally and totally. These were tears of joy, tears of release, tears of healing. In the years that followed I would become very familiar with these tears in the lives of the many who would come to me for healing prayer.

This experience opened up for me a whole new intimacy in prayer. Sentiments of praise and glory, thanksgiving and adoration began to flow spontaneously from my heart. Now I could relate to St. Paul's experiences and became attracted to his letters for the first time. His words and the entire Scripture had new meaning and force. In the months that followed I read everything I could lay my hands on to satisfy this hunger I had for the word of God. The reality of Jesus, risen and triumphant, began to fill my being. Now I understood what St. Paul meant when he described the indwelling of Christ as "the glory beyond price." He wrote to the Colossians: "God has willed to make known to them the glory beyond price which this mystery brings to the Gentiles – the mystery of Christ in you, your hope and glory" (Col. 1:27). To the Philippians, Paul would declare: "For, to me, `life' means Christ; hence dying is so much gain" (Phil. 1:21). These powerful proclamations of the transforming presence of Christ are for Paul the work of the Holy Spirit as he indicates in 1 Cor. 12:3: "And no one can say: `Jesus is Lord,' except in the Holy Spirit." The verb "say" here obviously means far more than speaking words. It means to proclaim from the conviction of experience what his encounter with the Risen Christ wrought in his personal life and in his ministry. Together with our personal transformation and renewal in Christ, the Holy Spirit pours out gifts on us for the enrichment of the Body. St. Paul mentions these in 1Cor. 12:4ff:

> To each person the manifestation of the Spirit is given for the common good. To one the Spirit

gives wisdom in discourse, to another the power to express knowledge. Through the Spirit one receives faith; by the same Spirit another is given the gift of healing, and still another miraculous powers. Prophecy is given to one; to another power to distinguish one spirit from another. One receives the gift of tongues, another the gift of interpreting the tongues. But it is one and the same Spirit who produces all these gifts, distributing them to each as he wills.

After his spiritual awakening, Father Michael Scanlon went on to revolutionize the Franciscan University at Steubenville. It is now perhaps the most Catholic Christian institution of learning in the world where virtually all of the students attend daily Mass, spend time before the Blessed Sacrament, pray the Rosary together daily, and live in a truly spiritual community environment.

Since the time of her dramatic healing at that retreat in Florida in 1970 and her Baptism in the Holy Spirit, Sr. Briege has become internationally known for her healing ministry and her special ministry to priests. She travels the world to bring the message of conversion, healing, and renewal to her spell-bound audiences. As with Peter's mother-in-law, she was raised up to serve the Church, and she does it with wonderful simplicity yet with amazing power.

Over the years I have seen these wonderful gifts being used to bring riches and healing to the members of our Church. While it is great to witness so many using their gifts today, it is true to say that most of our gifts are still dormant and perhaps will never be used to nurture the Body. Take the story of Father Luke from Australia who visited us some years ago. He did not know anything about gifts until his twenty-fifth anniversary of ordination. He returned to his home from New Guinea for the celebration after which he attended a Life in the Spirit seminar. The experience of Baptism in the Holy Spirit released this amazing gift of healing that lay hidden all those years.

Meet Father Emiliano Tardif. He was miraculously healed by charismatic prayer in his native Canada. This experience led him to full involvement in a dynamic international ministry of healing, deliverance, and evangelism.

Meet Brian Casey, a member of Good News International – a team of gifted laymen dedicated to the ministry of evangelization, both in this country and abroad. Brian was a highly successful lawyer and salesman in Seattle, WA, grossing $30,000 per month. He experienced conversion and a call to use his giftedness in proclaiming the Gospel. He gave away his wealth and now depends on the free-will offerings of those to whom he ministers. His witness has been truly inspirational to me and indeed to all who hear him.

Now meet a sister in Christ with an extraordinary story of conversion. You will meet her again, as a witness on the Eucharist in Chapter Nine.

In April of 1990 my husband and I vacationed in Arizona. I was eager to go because at this time in my life I was immersed in the New Age Movement [a false spirituality], and Sedona, at that time, was a town known for this movement. I embraced all that I considered New Age.

On my last day of vacation, I was reclining by the swimming pool [my husband was in the water] and a palm branch was over my head. Unexpectedly, a dove so brilliant white and surrounded by light hovered over me for about 12 seconds. Then the dove was gone. Immediately I jumped into the swimming pool and tears began to pour out of me. My husband asked me what was wrong, what happened, and I answered, "I don't know. All I know is I am not afraid anymore," and I was filled with a peace I have never known. This was my Metanoia, a gift from God to His child who had given up on Him and His Church and walked away from Him 20 years ago.

Immediately upon my return from Sedona, I destroyed all the New Age materials [books, tapes, etc.] I had and ended all communications with a New Age seer. The Lord led me to a very religious woman who founded a lay Marian community. I was praying with her when the Holy Spirit blessed me with the gift of tongues and other gifts to glorify Him. She confirmed it was the outpouring of the Holy Spirit and suggested I begin reading and pondering the scriptures daily and journaling what the Holy Spirit reveals. By the power and gifts of the Holy Spirit, I continue to do so even now, almost 30 years later.

Throughout the years the Holy Spirit has guided me on the spiritual journey He has planned for me; transforming, and healing so as to use me as He wills. The Holy Spirit has sent me in His perfect timing to serve in evangelization ministry, missionary work, faith formation, healing ministry, and more. In more recent years, He withdrew me from the more active and busy ministries, and as confirmed by several spiritual directors, guided me into contemplative prayer. My ministry now is to be a house of prayer, and in silence with the Lord within He shows me what to pray. "Holy Spirit, Love Divine, glow within this heart of mine; enkindle every high desire and perish all that is of self, in Thy pure fire."

How many more persons will follow in the footsteps of Father Philip, Father Michael, Father Luke, Father Emiliano, Sr. Briege, Brian Casey, the witness just above, and the many other inspirational witnesses to Gospel life that we have been privileged to know and work with through the years? We pray that there will be many whose glory stories are still waiting to be told as they continue the privileged work of building up the Body of Christ. How many of our wonderful priests, religious, and laity are struggling to serve the Lord while extraordinary gifts of the Holy Spirit lay dormant within them? What can we do to awaken these sleeping giants of giftedness in our Church? Yes, there is so much more if only we are open to the wonderful Spirit of God!

Has Baptism in the Holy Spirit affected my ministry? It certainly has. As the Spirit releases the gifts of Baptism and Confirmation, as he blesses us with a new intensity of love in the Holy Eucharist, he also unlocks the mystery of priesthood in a very profound way. I have been opened to a new focus and vitality in my ministry. I have experienced the love and mercy of Christ in the Sacrament of Reconciliation. I have seen penitents who were shackled with anger, fear, guilt, and shame become transformed and set free in this gentle, tender yet powerful encounter. I have seen dramatic healings in the Sacrament of the Anointing of the Sick, but the most common thread is a deep sense of peace and a healing of tension, fear, and worry, paving the way for healing, or preparing the person for the ultimate healing – death. I have come to accept as ordinary the power of Christ flowing from my hands when I pray over people for whatever need. I have accepted my powerlessness and have become comfortable surrendering every need that comes my way to the infinite power of Christ. He always works as he wishes, in so many beautiful ways, to bring his salvation and healing love to his children. I never cease to be amazed at this and pray that he may continue to use me in whatever manner he desires to build up his Body, the Church.

Charismatic Renewal is a wonderful gift of the Holy Spirit to the Church in the twentieth and twenty-first centuries. For those who are open, extraordinary happenings of early Church caliber have almost become the ordinary. Yet there is much misunderstanding, mistrust, and skepticism afloat. Our call today is to be obedient to the Spirit and to faithfully bring the message of renewal to all who serve the Church. In an age when the Church is suffering so painfully from lack of vocations, stress, over-work, frustration, anger, division, and scandal, it is surely time to pray for a new Pentecost and in faith expect the powerful Spirit of God to once again dramatically renew the Church and indeed the face of the earth.

In his September 1993 address to some charismatic retreatants returned from Assisi, Pope John Paul II reflected on renewal and offered it his blessing:

> These great figures of holiness in the Church (St. Francis and St. Clare) made their own the words of St. Paul: "It is no longer I who live, but Christ who lives in me" (Gal. 2:20). Is this not the ideal and goal which permeates the Charismatic Renewal? Is it not the program of life which your prayer groups and communities have set for themselves under the guidance of the Holy Spirit? May the example and the intercession of the saints of Assisi strengthen your resolve to grow continually in evangelical love and service "to the measure and stature of the fullness of Christ" (Eph. 4:13).

FIVE

Bringing the Baptism in the Holy Spirit to the Heart of the Church

In the late eighties, the substance of this chapter was published in *Hearts of Flame*, our publication that back then served the Charismatic community in our Diocese and beyond.

The central focus of the Charismatic Movement is not charisms. This may sound like a contradiction in terms, yet it is the truth. This does not mean that charisms are not important — all of God's gifts are indeed very important for the spread of the Gospel and the building up of the Body of Christ. However, the focus and thrust of the movement is, as our masthead motto stated, to bring the Baptism in the Holy Spirit to the heart of the Church. While the Charismatic Movement has been leading men and women of the Church to experience the Baptism in the Holy Spirit for over thirty years back then, and had changed the lives of over one hundred million Catholics, there is still a dearth of understanding in the body of the Church as to the nature and scope of this experience.

We are pleased to bring you part of an excellent presentation on the Baptism in the Holy Spirit by Father Raniero Cantalamessa, OFM, internationally known theologian and preacher to the Papal Household. We hope that it will offer substantial enlightenment and help the reader to articulate more clearly the working of the Holy Spirit in the Church in our time.

Many years back the National Service Committee of the Charismatic Renewal published an important document called *Fanning the Flame*. The aim of the document was, in the words of Bishop Sam Jacobs in his introductory letter, "to initiate further theological reflections on the question of the grace of Pentecost, to bring people into the fuller awareness of God's plan for all His people and to encourage the development of models by wise, pastoral Church leaders for the implementation of the underlying premise of the document, namely, that being fully baptized in the Holy Spirit is part of the public, liturgical life of the Church."

Even as the Renewal Movement's leaders embarked on this lofty mission of introducing all of the faithful to the experience of the Baptism in the Holy Spirit, they were quick to point out that this experience was not unique to Charismatic Renewal. The document clearly stated:

> Baptism in the Holy Spirit is captive to no camp, whether liberal or conservative. Nor is it identified with any movement, nor with any style of prayer, worship or community. On the contrary, we believe that the gift of the baptism in the Holy Spirit belongs to the Christian inheritance of all those sacramentally initiated into the Church.

It is clear then that the Charismatic Movement is the work of the Holy Spirit in the Church as primarily one of transformation and sanctification through Baptism,

Confirmation, and Eucharist. This action of the Spirit can only come to fuller fruition in our adult lives when we seek a deeper conversion to Christ and are open and docile to the Holy Spirit's lead. This is the vocation of all Christians, not the isolated few. Baptism in the Holy Spirit is therefore for all of the faithful, where together we can all cry out from the depth of spiritual conviction that *Jesus Christ is Lord*. The first Pentecost and the lived experience of the early Church all point to dramatic changes in the adult converts when they experienced Baptism and Confirmation. Not only were they ontologically transformed into the very life of the Holy Trinity, they actually experienced that inner transformation and anointing. They began to manifest this anointing in gifts of adoration and praise, and in a deep awareness of the presence of the Risen Christ in their hearts. They were drawn into an intense communion of love where the needs of all, both spiritual and temporal, were attended to. There was generated an intense desire to share this newfound faith experience: evangelization was moving into high gear. Then there were the manifestations of the charisms, prophecy, tongues, healings, etc. that accompanied the preaching of the Gospel.

Today, the Church looks to a new evangelization, a new springtime of Christian life. For this mission she needs once again a powerful anointing of the Holy Spirit that will be manifest in lives that are radically changed, set on fire for the Gospel and living in faith community that is characterized by intense love, generosity, and hospitality. Here the Church will be seen as home for all, even the most isolated and downcast. It is precisely this manifest love and quality of life that will draw men and women to the Church. On the contrary, the sobering response of Friedrich Nietzsche, to those who asked why he was not Christian, should resonate with all of us: "Christians would have to look more redeemed for me to believe in their Redeemer."

It is through Baptism in the Holy Spirit, that immersion in Divine Love, Life and Community, that the Christian Community manifests to the world that Jesus is Lord, that He is alive in His Church and is drawing all men and women to Himself. Let us continue to seek a deeper immersion and more radical transformation so that we will be empowered to fulfill our evangelical mission to the world.

In preparing for the annual Charismatic Conference in Atlantic City in 1974, a Scripture from the prophet Ezekiel was highlighted in the invitation brochure that really touched my heart. From these verses we can see why Ezekiel was called the prophet of regeneration:

> For I will take you out of the nations; I will gather you from all the countries and bring you back into your own land. I will sprinkle clean water on you, and you will be clean; I will cleanse you from all your impurities and from all your idols. I will give you a new heart and put a new spirit in you; I will remove from you your heart of stone and give you a heart of flesh. And I will put my Spirit in you and move you to follow my decrees and be careful to keep my laws. Then you will live in the

land I gave your ancestors; you will be my people, and I will be your God (Ez. 36:24-28).

Preceding these verses in chapter 34, Ezekiel foreshadows Christ the Good Shepherd.

I will tend them in a good pasture, and the mountain heights of Israel will be their grazing land. There they will lie down in good grazing land, and there they will feed in a rich pasture on the mountains of Israel. I myself will tend my sheep and have them lie down, declares the Sovereign Lord. I will search for the lost and bring back the strays. I will bind up the injured and strengthen the weak, but the sleek and the strong I will destroy. I will shepherd the flock with justice (Ez. 34:14-16).

Zechariah also foresees Christ as the Good Shepherd: "The Lord their God will save his people on that day as a shepherd saves his flock. They will sparkle in his land like jewels in a crown" (9:16). In the Gospels, Jesus will recall Ezekiel's prophecies in showing that he is their fulfillment: "I am the good shepherd. The good shepherd lays down his life for his sheep" (Jn. 10:11). "I am the good shepherd; I know my sheep and my sheep know me" (Jn. 10:14).

Why is the shepherd chosen as a model for Christ? The shepherd lived with his sheep. He knew them by name. He loved them, cared for them, led them to the green grass and fresh waters. He guarded them from the wild beasts and robbers. He never left them and was with them day and night. When a sheep wandered from the fold and got lost he would leave the fold and bring the lost one back on his shoulders. Because of these qualities, his sheep trusted him totally and they would follow him wherever he would lead.

When we open our hearts to Christ through the power of the Holy Spirit coming from his Sacred Heart, we have the experience of total love and caring. It is this total love that now generates total trust on our part. We are nurtured by his word and sacrament and the riches of theological and spiritual literature. We are ennobled through sacred music, sacred art, and architecture that the Holy Spirit has brought us through our wonderful saints, scholars, artists, architects, and builders. We are enriched by the spiritual legacy of our evangelists and missionaries who over the centuries brought us the message of the Gospel and still are by our sides encouraging us as we make our journey together to be with them forever in the arms of our Father in Heaven.

In the Church we are also truly enriched by the spiritual communion with our brothers and sisters who are on this journey with us. I must say, with a deep sense of gratitude, that I have been deeply blessed and inspired in sharing and receiving the spiritual intimacy that communion in the Body of Christ brings us. Whenever I gave in ministry, I was always blessed and enriched tenfold. It has been a special privilege for me to work with many of the gifted saints who enrich, or have enriched, our Church in the godly work of evangelization and other areas of ministry.

There is a document on Baptism in the Holy Spirit, published by International Catholic Charismatic Renewal Services, Doctrinal Commission, that I would highly recommend to all our Catholic community. Its first chapter, "The Characteristics and Fruits of Baptism in the Holy Spirit", begins thus:

> Baptism in the Holy Spirit is a life-transforming experience of the love of God the Father poured into one's heart by the Holy Spirit, received through a surrender through the lordship of Christ. It brings alive sacramental baptism and confirmation, deepens communion with God and with fellow Christians, enkindles evangelistic fervor and equips a person with charisms for service and mission.

This statement summarizes what we ourselves have experienced in our personal encounters with the Holy Spirit. We too have been transformed in mind and heart with overwhelming divine love, empowered with gifts that we never knew we had, brought into an intimate communion with the Holy Trinity and with all of the Body of Christ.

We have experienced the Sacraments and the Word of God as power and light. We have been truly surprised at the emergence of charismatic gifts such as discernment, healing, words of knowledge, and deliverance of evil spirits. We have experienced a greater love and understanding especially for those who despise and even hate us. We have become more and more sensitive to the presence of evil spirits and their destructive powers.

For those in ministry, we have experienced our Liturgical celebrations and our preaching more engaging and fruitful, and our ministry in the Confessional more effective. I have been blessed to have been called to preach and teach and bring healing in my ministry as a High School Chaplain for four years, followed by ministry as Pastor for thirty-three years. In addition, I felt called to preach, teach, and minister overseas several times in Ireland, in Slovakia, the Czech Republic, Jamaica, and China.

The blessings and fruits of those missions were truly great, thanks to the work of the Holy Spirit for using us to bring the love of God our Father and the fruits of Jesus' love that came to us through the Cross. And it all was made possible primarily through the Baptism in the Spirit.

SIX

Divine Mercy, Forgiveness, and Healing

Mercy has been at the heart of the Good News from the dawn of human history. With the fall of our First Parents, it was our Heavenly Father's plan to redeem humanity in the ultimate act of mercy, brought about by the incarnation, passion, death, and resurrection of Jesus, His own beloved Son. Here we see mercy at its greatest. However, we will see the word "mercy" appear often in the Scriptures over the centuries, in fact, one hundred and twenty-six times. It will be listed as mercy sought, mercy offered, mercy given, and mercy refused. It will be promoted as one of the greatest forms of love that is intimately connected with forgiveness and the cancelling of debts that are especially the result of serious sin.

In our time we are very fortunate to see how Our Savior, Jesus Christ, has brought to the fore through St. Faustina the Divine Mercy Movement that has become a world-wide drive to prepare humanity for salvation as we face the end times.

Here are Our Savior's words coming to us through St. Faustina:

> I demand from you deeds of mercy, you must not shrink from this or try to excuse or absolve yourself from it. I give you three ways of exercising

mercy, the first by deed, the second by word, and the third by prayer. In these three degrees is contained the fullness of mercy, and it is an unquestionable proof of love for Me. By these means a soul glorifies and pays reverence to My mercy (*Diary of Saint Faustina,* 742).

What an appropriate way to begin our chapter on Forgiveness and Healing and Mercy. The message that Jesus gave to St. Faustina is one of complete love and mercy for poor sinners and for every soul that will draw near to Him. "My mercy is greater than your sins, and those of the entire world." He says, "I will let my Sacred Heart be pierced with a lance, thus opening wide the source of mercy for you. Come with trust to draw graces from this fountain." Jesus calls upon us to trust Him, to receive His mercy and to let it flow to others. "No soul that has called upon my Mercy has ever been disappointed" (Divine Mercy Leaflet).

Mike was a warm and jovial Irishman from my native County Kerry. Our common heritage gave us a natural bond and offered much familiar ground for warm and lively exchanges when we got together. However, our deepest and most memorable encounters always centered on the Lord and the transforming power of the Holy Spirit. Mike had been baptized in the Holy Spirit back in the late sixties and had been active in renewal ever since. His warmth and wit, anointed by the loving flame of the Spirit, were infectious and brought a spirit of joy, love, and genuine Christian friendship wherever Mike went.

I feel very fortunate indeed to have had the privilege of sharing his faith and friendship and of being enriched by the wisdom that flowed from his lived experience of the Gospel. One lesson he taught me I will never forget. I was on one occasion a dinner guest at his home and, as was always the case with Mike and his wife Mary, the conversation turned to spiritual matters. He shared his experiences in Charismatic Renewal and how the Holy Spirit had changed his life. He had come to know many of the well-known leaders and recalled his inner journey that brought about deep spiritual transformation and many healings. One affliction, however, that he could not discard was a heavy addiction to nicotine. Despite numerous prayer sessions with some of the most gifted people in the healing ministry, he was still trapped in a three-pack-a-day habit. While he experienced God's love in so many areas of his life, he was at a loss to explain why his Lord seemed to ignore his pleas in this one area.

One night he and some friends were in prayer and suddenly one of the participants received a word of knowledge. He saw Mike as a youth in Ireland deeply hurt by a teacher. Then it all came back. Mike was a student at the Christian Brothers High School in Tralee. At that time smoking was strictly prohibited on the campus, but that did not deter some students from taking chances. One day during lunch period as Mike was sneaking a cigarette in the handball alley, one of the Brothers came upon him and gave him a severe beating and then proceeded to humiliate him before the class. Mike developed an intense hatred for that Brother for the remainder of his high school years and never forgave him.

As the years passed, he forgot about the incident and went on with his life. However, forgetting did not delete the memory – it simply buried it alive. The buried memory now was transformed into an addiction to the very substance that occasioned the altercation in the first place – nicotine. As this memory was awakened before his eyes, Mike got on his knees and forgave that Brother. He repented his sin of hatred and resentment and begged God to forgive him. Then the group gathered around him and prayed for an infilling of the Holy Spirit to cleanse the infection of that memory and break the shackles of addiction that resulted from it. Immediately Mike felt the healing balm of our Father's unconditional love. He was set free and he had smoked his last cigarette.

I was deeply moved by this sharing. Somehow my eyes were being opened to a new level of Gospel wisdom and power. Through my human vision I had seen much of the Sermon on the Mount as an obstacle course that was meant to test the fiber of Christians and cause religion's version of natural selection. Now I began to realize that forgiveness was not part of an endurance test but a necessary means to health – spiritual, emotional and oftentimes even physical. In all of my studies of psychology I had never seen forgiveness promoted as an essential in the stages of therapy. It seems that the wisdom of the Gospel eluded Freud and his followers too. It is not surprising then that there is so little real healing in secular models of therapy. As my former professor of Basic Psychiatry warned us when I began graduate studies in 1969, psychotherapy's goal was not to heal, its aim was to help patients cope and become functional in society. The goal of counseling was to help people develop higher level adjustment skills. "Higher level adjustment skills" undoubtedly add to the healing process but cannot take the place of that bedrock sense of wholeness that comes from the liberating and empowering love of Christ.

My early efforts at counseling were, in all honesty, a failure. Not only was very little visible good being done for my clients, but I was becoming emotionally exhausted in vain attempts to put into practice what I had learned. Three years later, in 1975, my whole outlook and ministry would change after I experienced Baptism in the Holy Spirit. Catholic Charismatic Renewal opened up to me a new world of spiritual experiences that included a healing ministry unlike anything I had witnessed in my studies. The writings of Kathryn Kuhlman, Agnes Sanford, Francis MacNutt, and others' testimonies, which I was hearing at conferences and prayer groups, and the recent reform of the Sacrament of the Anointing of the Sick (1974) all indicated that the healing ministry of Christ was coming back in full force through His Church. This was a source of great joy to me, knowing that Jesus' love could be touched in such a concrete way as in the witness of a healing. Francis MacNutt reflected my inner feeling in his well-known book, *Healing.* "I believe that the ministry of healing is what lifts the central doctrine of redemption and salvation from the realm of the abstract into the reality of men's lives. One of the greatest losses the Church has suffered has been her full heritage of healing power" (33). Now this "full heritage" was becoming again the ordinary heritage of the Baptized.

As people were being baptized in the Holy Spirit, they were experiencing an inner transformation that made Jesus real, alive and present. The Word of God was taking on a new force and meaning that was truly life-giving and enriching. Jesus' powers to save and heal were now seen as flowing from the same source – the fruits of His Cross and Resurrection, now bestowed as gifts to the Church to be shared and celebrated.

While this was exciting good news for me, it also brought with it a certain inner panic. It meant that I would have to adjust my approach to ministry and take a step out in faith. I was accustomed to praying for people. This was indeed a good and beneficial practice, but it allowed me to remain distant and in control. If nothing happened, we could always chalk it up to God's will and go on with life. Interiorly now I was being moved to pray with people. This was a scary move. I was no longer removed and in control. When I prayed with someone, I was called to surrender, admitting that the Holy Spirit was in charge. I can still remember those first sessions of uncertainty and helplessness, waiting on the Holy Spirit to do His work. Yet, reaching this point of helplessness was the necessary step in faith to connect with the awesome power of God. Almost immediately things began to happen. Not only were people experiencing the Lord's healing love, I myself was being touched by it. Gone was that emotional fatigue that was so familiar in my counseling days; I was now being refreshed and renewed when I surrendered in prayer to the healing power of Christ. The words of Proverbs were indeed being fulfilled for me, "He who confers benefits will be amply enriched and he who refreshes others will himself be refreshed" (11:25).

Healings did not come in any one pattern. The Holy Spirit moves as He wills. However, as I always experienced His reassuring presence when I prayed, my anxieties soon diminished and my trust in His gentle, healing love grew. Due to the nature of the illness, the client's disposition, and a number of other intangibles, progress varied. The initial prayer would open us up to the love of Christ as revealed by the Holy Spirit. As the person began to experience this love, the way was being gently paved to openness and trust. This would lead to the courage needed to face one's sins and the deep-rooted hurts of life. Opening up this inner pain is a form of emotional surgery that unravels intense feelings of rage, anger, rejection, self-hatred, self-destruction, guilt, shame, bitterness, and a host of other related painful feelings. At this point we would "bathe" these wounds in the Wounds of Christ so that the client would find courage and strength to go on to the next step which is forgiveness. I would remind them that it was when Jesus hung from the Cross in His excruciating pain that He forgave His enemies. It was here that He gave us the eminent example of practicing what He preached, "You have heard that it was said, 'You shall love your neighbor and hate your enemy.' But I say to you, love your enemies, and pray for those who persecute you, that you may be children of your heavenly Father, for he makes the sun rise on the bad and the good, and causes rain to fall on the just and unjust" (Mt. 5:43-45).

We must remember that this kind of forgiveness does not come naturally; it is not a product of the flesh. It is through the power of the Holy Spirit that we can let our enemies go and surrender them to the mercy of Christ. This act of forgiveness must be an act of the will that flows from the depths of the heart precisely as the person is experiencing again the uncovered pain and hurt. To ensure that it is an act of the heart and not just a mental exercise, I take them through a special faith imagination exercise. We put ourselves in the presence of Christ, Who has promised to be with those who gather in His name (Mt. 18:20). We visualize Jesus knocking at the door of our heart and calling us by name. We go to the door, open it, and invite Jesus. We allow Him to embrace and love us and breathe on us the Holy Spirit so that the healing process can get under way. We then ask Jesus to take us on a journey back in life to the hurtful memories that He wants to heal in the person's life. When we are brought face to face with the person who hurt us, we allow the inner pain to resurface once again.

I explain that when we are hurt it is as if we are bound in chains. However, bound at the other end of the chain is the person who hurt us. They are victims of their own aggression. The process of forgiveness then is to have the victim visualize these chains of bondage. Since the power to forgive is a gift of the Holy Spirit, we visualize it in the form of a golden key that Jesus gives us. The act of forgiveness then is acted out as the patient goes to the aggressor, unlocks the padlock, removes the chain, and surrenders him or her to the merciful embrace of Jesus. The patient now begins to realize that he too is freed from the chains. We will then ask Jesus to fill all the inner wounds with His healing love. What follows is an exhilarating feeling of freedom and well-being. The painful memories are transformed into moments of loving, divine intervention where Jesus entered and set the captives free. (Lk. 4:18-19).

I remember a couple that came to see me who were preparing for marriage. I explained the whole process involved in the healing ministry. We must face the hurts of the past so that we can grow together in trust that may have been shattered in previous relationships.

The hit song by Hank Williams, Sr., "Cold, Cold Heart" gives us a very realistic example of the tragedy that the hurts of a former broken relationship will bring, if not healed, to future interpersonal encounters. This is especially true for those attempting marriage:

> I tried so hard, my dear, to show that you're my every dream
> Yet you're afraid each thing I do is just some evil scheme.
> A memory from your lonesome past keeps us so far apart
> Why can't I free your doubtful mind and melt your cold, cold heart?
>
> Another love before my time made your heart sad and blue
> And so my heart is paying for the things I didn't do
> In anger, unkind words are said that make the teardrops start
> Why can't I free your doubtful mind and melt your cold, cold heart?

I shared these verses once with a couple who came to see me. They were preparing for marriage. Immediately I sensed tension rising in the future bride. They did not come back again. I have prayed for that couple and indeed many others who were not open to the healing power of Christ that comes in the Holy Spirit through forgiveness and healing.

On the brighter side we have another testimony that demonstrates the wonderful blessing of divine healing:

> After all my years of professional counseling, I have never felt the peace or total renewal as I felt when I left your office. Since I've seen you my attitude has completely changed and I feel that the overbearing feelings of depression, anxiety, and guilt only remain in the slightest bit. It still remains a mystery to me how one hour can change my way of life and my thinking, but I guess the mystery of God is hard for any of us to understand as earthly beings. We just have to believe...The day after the first day of the rest of my life! After the experience I had with you yesterday, it is hard to know where it has left you, but I want you to know, this experience has really nourished my inner soul. Thank you for being a brother in Christ Jesus to me, and for assisting me to receive a healing in faith which is bringing me to a new level of knowing the Lord and walking one with the Lord. It was the most difficult task for me to expose and disclose some of my very personal issues, but with the Lord's love it became very easy. Praise God from whom all blessings flow! — M.

The healing steps we followed in these instances are valid in every situation. Take the situation of a woman who has had an abortion. The first step is that she confesses her sin in the Sacrament of Reconciliation. She forgives all those who hurt her in life. Through Jesus, she asks her aborted child for forgiveness. She receives back her mother relationship that she discarded in the intention and act of abortion. She acknowledges that her child is a person by giving a name that is applicable to either gender (in many cases in which I have ministered, the mothers seemed to have known whether it was a boy or girl). In prayer we surrender the child to Jesus and ask Him to baptize the child in His Precious Blood and receive him or her as one of the Holy Innocents. The final stage in healing the effects of abortion is often the most difficult, self-forgiveness. Again, so that it becomes an event of the heart, I ask her to visualize herself at the time of the abortion and to go to that young woman, with the compassion of Jesus, and unlock the chains of bondage. Since forgiveness of all others who have caused her hurt has to come first, we make sure that all of her offenders are unchained and surrendered to the Lord. As she completes these stages, it is then that the merciful love of Christ begins to flow in this mother's heart that was filled with guilt, shame, regret, and remorse.

However, getting to the stage of self-forgiveness is very difficult, so we have to work with patience to complete that step. I have her visualize the door of the dungeon where she has locked away the younger self and thrown away the key. Now she asks Jesus for his golden key of forgiveness. She now unlocks the dungeon and gently takes that broken self and leads her out. She can now forgive her, and in turn ask her for forgiveness for the act of self-condemnation. Then she leads her to Jesus and

Mary for the embrace of their unconditional and perfect love.

We lay hands on her head and pray for an infilling of the Holy Spirit. It is here also that we will quietly pray for deliverance of any evil spirits who may have entered along the way: spirits of lust, death, self-destruction, condemnation, etc. The result is a deep sense of divine peace and freedom, of gratitude, and rebirth. It will also lead to outreach in prayer and ministry for other women who have gone the way of abortion or are considering it. Some of our great leaders in the pro-life cause today are women who have been through the abortion experience themselves, or may even have been abortion providers at one time. Praise the Lord for his awesome mercy and love.

Here is a testimony of a woman who has been through the mill and is now willing to share her story with us:

My father died unexpectedly when I was thirty-two. We had always been close and I clung to him as a child. My reaction to his death was the painful thought that no one would ever love me as he did. I was devastated. However my father's death led me on a journey back to the faith of my youth.

I had been raised a Catholic and gone to Catholic grammar school. However, I lost that faith in college and didn't practice the sacraments for years. I was busy at work and raising children, so I told myself that I didn't have time for church. That was far from the truth. I was afraid.

As a young woman, I had gotten involved with an older man and found myself pregnant and deserted. In fear, I had an abortion. At first, I was relieved, but then the overwhelming guilt and shame set in. I pushed the pain and regret down, and tried to carry on but it came out in other ways. I always felt unworthy of love. I ate too much and smoked. I had a problem accepting the love of others. I knew I had to go to God but my fear of rejection overwhelmed me.

Finally, the burden of that sin led me to the belief that I had to go back to the Church and confession. Still the fear of rejection and shame kept me in limbo. Each Saturday, I would drive to my local church and sit in my car in the parking lot. I would watch people coming out of confession. But I would drive away, unable to go inside.

Finally, I found the courage to go inside and enter the confessional. I explained that I had forgotten the prayers and the priest helped me. I blurted out my mortal sin and fully expected I would be asked to leave and never come back. Instead, I heard the priest say, "Welcome back, prodigal daughter."

Those words changed my life. I was forgiven. I believed that my sin was wiped away and I was in God's grace. Still, I found myself crying all the time. Every time I heard the song (my favorite song) "Be Not Afraid," I had to leave the church because of uncontrollable weeping. This went on for a year.

Finally, I attended a Life in the Spirit Seminar. I had no idea how powerful the moment of my Baptism would be. The priest laid his hands on my head and I felt a powerful infilling of the Holy Spirit. I also heard the internal words, "I have forgiven you, now forgive yourself."

It is easy for me to forgive others, but hard for me to forgive myself when I make a mistake or commit a sin. I realized that while God had forgiven me, I still carried that guilt and pain in my heart because I didn't have the ability to forgive myself. I asked God to give me the grace I needed to have mercy on the young, frightened girl I had been. Not only was I able to forgive myself in that moment of Baptism, I was given the gift of joy. It was the greatest gift of my life. I forgave myself in the power of the Holy Spirit and never cried over that sin again. I found joy in the song that always made me cry. I find joy in all circumstances in my life. I accept God's forgiveness and have never looked back. The words "Be Not Afraid" are branded on my heart. — T.

Thanks so much, T., for this sharing. We pray that it will be read by other women and become a source of encouragement for them to come forth and know the power of divine mercy in forgiveness and healing.

The end results of forgiveness and healing are expressed in joy, deep inner freedom, and a sense of well-being including a new outlook on life. We will also see a new vision of self, others, and especially God. As Christ's healing touch and the warm glow of the Holy Spirit bring forth a new inner life, we then pray for an empowerment to ministry. As with Peter's mother-in-law (Mt. 8:14), we are healed not just for our own well-being. We are now called to share this unconditional love and mercy of Christ with others. In fact, it seems to be part of God's plan to use the wounded and broken to be among His most powerful ministers of healing and evangelization once they have experienced His saving and healing touch.

Before I finish, let me bring you up to date lest my friends in the field of clinical psychology become angered at me. It seems that this august body has been playing catch-up with Gospel values, in its diverse fields, as is evident in the theme of a 1996 conference entitled "National Conference on Forgiveness in Clinical Practice". All we can say is: Thank God the word is out!

Now here is an ironic twist. Theologian Morton Kelsey has written a history of healing in the Church and claims that today medical doctors and psychiatrists are more open to healing prayer than clergy. He states, "Except for Pentecostal seminaries, we have found that, of the hundreds of Christian seminaries, less than half a dozen offer any courses in the religious dimensions of healing. In most seminaries the subject is dismissed with scorn" (Psychology, Medicine and Christian Healing, 3).

Here is yet another powerful testimony:

Dear Friend in Christ, I apologize for the impersonal nature of the typed note, but I really want to express my gratitude to you and am finding myself woefully short of words when I try to do it in person. Even in writing, my words fall short of the depth of gratitude that I have in my heart.

I lost so much due to the selfishness and infidelity of one priest – my innocence and purity, my love for the church, and most of all my relationship with the Lord. A part of my identity seemed to me to be irreparably damaged and the path of self-condemnation and self-punishment that I chose to walk on seemed irreversible. I praise and glorify the Lord for his love and mercy and the truth that He can "make all things new." I thank Him for building up in me a trust in Him that I thought was forever lost. I am in awe of the way He has worked in my life – continually and gently pulling his fearful, reluctant, and somewhat stubborn child out of darkness. And although I don't understand why He allowed certain things to happen in my life, I am at peace with the fact that He has and will continue to work out all things for my good and His glory.

As you pointed out to me in a way I had never considered before, the Lord began a beautiful restoration process in my life initially through Papa ten years ago in Rome, restoring my relationship with Him and giving me the grace to once again love his Church. However, He has surely continued it and to a great extent accomplished much of the messy, painful, detail-work of healing and growth through you.

Your unselfishness and fidelity to your priesthood has been a major instrument of healing and restoration in my life. I have never experienced anything but love in your eyes, compassion in your voice, and gentleness in your demeanor. Even in the most difficult moments of the "hot seat" for me – moments of overcoming some of my most paralyzing fears; moments of facing the ugly reality of abuse; moments of confessing my most shameful sins; even moments when I felt like what you were dispensing was "tough-love" – you have always made me feel encouraged and safe to take the next step in faith.

I thank you for your love and the way that the Love of Jesus radiates through you – no matter how uncomfortable, vulnerable, anxious, confused, or hurting I felt, those feelings were always enveloped and calmed by the atmosphere of love in your office. I thank you for your perseverance – I am certain that there are some essential truths about the Lord and also about what happened to me that you have spoken countless times, before I allowed them to penetrate the walls of my heart and mind. I thank you for your courage – without it I would never have been able to face the full horror of my experience and the full depth of my own pain. I thank you for your patience – because of it I am learning to be more patient with myself and others, and am slowly becoming comfortable with the fact that purification, healing, and the road to holiness is a lifelong journey. I thank you for your well-timed sense of humor which always eases tension, gives me permission to laugh at myself, and cools down the "hot seat" by at least 20 degrees or more! Most of all I thank you for your prayers – the effects of which I am sure I will understand very little of this side of eternity. The time I have spent on your "hot seat" and in your confessional has rarely been easy, but it has always been fruitful.

I continue to be amazed by the Lord's ways and wonder in awe at the mystery of them. In my wildest dreams I would never have imagined that the Lord would choose to heal the damage done to me by the sin of one priest through the goodness and love of another. I thank you for accompanying me and guiding me on my journey Home. I thank the Lord daily for the gift of you, and your priesthood. You are very special, and I am blessed beyond measure to know you.

What can I say in response to this letter but simply: Thank you, Lord, for making me an instrument of your healing, liberation, and peace to such a broken child of Yours. There is no greater joy, no greater sense of privilege, no greater sense of accomplishment, no greater honor, than to bring a child of God out of the dungeon of slavery and the shackles of brokenness and despair, to the sense of liberation, joy, and intimacy, of now living in the hearts of Father, Son, and Spirit, and the warmth and protection of the tender, maternal love, in the Immaculate Heart of Mary.

Another letter expresses the awesome gratitude to the Lord of Mercy that comes through the Sacrament of Reconciliation:

> Just a line to thank you for the most heartfelt and Spirit-filled weekend I had when you were with us. You opened up a whole new me, with the love and forgiveness that God the Father has for me. You, with the Holy Spirit working in you, set me free from my past. When I got ill this past year, my past has been coming before me, the sins of my past that I could not let go. Now I know that all is forgiven because, again, with the Holy Spirit working in you, God loves me and that Jesus is telling me to come, just as I am, into His care, and He in turn will bring me to the Father who will not hold my past against me.
>
> I thank God for your priesthood and how the Holy Spirit works in you. I felt that Jesus was talking to me when you spoke about Abba Father and about forgiveness and love. I now am free and feel safer. I am looking forward and not back over my past. God bless you, Father. Again I thank God for you. May God bless you, may Jesus walk with you, and may the Holy Spirit give you the courage to go on with your ministry. Yours in Christ, — D.

This is yet another response to the awesome power and love coming to us from the heart of Christ through the gentle working of the Holy Spirit. How awesome is our God who uses us, His weak and simple servants, to convey to others His infinite and tender love and healing.

> I cannot express the peace and love I feel since this afternoon's healing with you and my sister. When I looked into your eyes, I felt like I had known you for a thousand years. I saw the presence of a good soul! Through your love and faith, you have renewed my spirit. My tears shed so much pain and anguish. You will never know how accurate your message was to us; we were still prisoners of our childhoods. The Lord spoke through you – how blessed we are! Again, thank you for your love and healing. I thank God for you in my life. Sincerely, — J.

Thank you, Lord, for the power of Your healing love now flowing in the Church renewed each year. Thanks to all who have chosen to share the story of their ascent from brokenness and despair to the liberating and joy-filled experience of being now among the beloved children in the arms of Abba Father.

Our Holy Father asked us to make the year 2000 a special year of self-examination and conversion. This is a time of repentance, a time of forgiving and asking for forgiveness. It is a time of facing our sinfulness and dealing with our hurts. It is a year of openness and surrender to the Holy Spirit, Who will prepare us to encounter more deeply the three Persons of the Holy Trinity over the years ahead. With Mary as our model of anticipation, let us prepare for a future with expectant joy and hope, and the assurance of faith that when we embrace the Gospel we are entering into the highest quality of life possible on this earth, which is only a shadow of the life of heaven.

SEVEN

The Holy Spirit, the Evangelizer

Some years back I received an email from a student in one of our Catholic High Schools. He was really excited and not in the least hesitant in sharing his love for the Lord. He was designing a Catholic website for youth and was praying for the evangelization of his school – both faculty and students. With enthusiasm he related that the Holy Spirit was already at work. They had begun Eucharistic Adoration once a month. He related how an Evangelical Lutheran classmate was now praying the Rosary, and a born-again Christian friend was coming to Eucharistic Adoration. He wrote that at adoration his friend had "been touched by the true and awesome presence of Our Lord Jesus!" Each morning he invited students to come to Mass with him. His gentle persistence paid off as more students were now beginning to join him.

What made this young man so special? Where did this fire for evangelization come from? The answer: The Holy Spirit. A few years ago he attended a seminar and was baptized in the Holy Spirit. Since then his whole outlook had changed. He had developed a deep love for the Lord and treasured the time he spent in our Eucharistic Chapel. He loved the Church and wanted to give his life in the service of the Gospel. Indeed, he is an eloquent example of how the Holy Spirit works in the life and ministry of the Church. He is what Vatican II had in mind when it developed the role of the laity in the Church's mission to evangelize the world.

For me, the emergence of an awareness among the laity of their exalted role in evangelization by reason of their Baptism is one of the most exciting developments of our time. I venture to say that when this awareness becomes universally accepted and lived we will see an extraordinary explosion in our Church and the possibility of preaching the Gospel to every person on the face of the earth will become a virtual reality.

The Second Vatican Council has paved the way for empowering the laity in the mission of the Church. The Council Fathers went out of their way to redefine the nature and role of the baptized. It was the first Council to speak of the priesthood of the laity. In fact, it used the term "priesthood" exclusively in reference to the baptized. To define the ministerial priesthood, it used the term "presbyterate". This showed that it was returning to biblical roots to reestablish the true role of the laity in the mission of the Church. In the New Testament, there are only four references to priesthood, and they all refer to the common priesthood of the baptized: 1 Peter 2:5,9; Rev. 1:5-6, 5:9-10, 20:6.

In *Lumen Gentium* the Council Fathers tell us that all the baptized share in the priesthood of Jesus Christ and they go on to say that, "The faithful join in the offering of the Eucharist by virtue of their royal priesthood" and exercise that priesthood, "by the witness of a holy life, and by self-denial and acts of charity" (10:2).

The Council develops this common priesthood further in the context of evangelization in the *Decree on the Apostolate of the Laity*. In paragraph 3 it states,

> From the fact of their union with Christ the head, flows the layman's right and duty to be an apostle. Inserted as they are into the Mystical Body of Christ by baptism and strengthened by the power of the Holy Spirit in confirmation, it is by the Lord himself that they are assigned to the apostolate. If they are consecrated a kingly priesthood and a holy nation (cf. 1 Pet. 2:4-10), it is in order that they may in all their actions offer spiritual sacrifices and bear witness to Christ all the world over.

Clearly then the laity receive their call from Baptism to be evangelists and missionaries for the Gospel. This reality is beginning to take shape in our Church today with many excellent lay men and women responding to their baptismal vocation and using their wonderful gifts for the spread of the Kingdom. It would be an exaggeration to think that using our gifts means always entering into a specialized ministry. The fact is that the vast majority of our empowered Catholics will continue in their regular jobs or professions but will find ample opportunities to give witness by holy lives and by sharing their faith story whenever the occasion arises. My own experience in the various elements of renewal convinces me that our greatest pastoral efforts today should be directed to empowering our laity in their baptismal mission and offering them every opportunity to use their God-given gifts to enrich the Church and spread the Gospel.

Is there an inherent danger then that by emphasizing the common priesthood we will de-emphasize or obscure the presbyterate? Theoretically that could happen. But it has not been my experience thus far; in fact, the opposite is the case on two counts. For me, renewal in the Holy Spirit and the discovery of the riches of my baptismal gifts has only enhanced and enriched my presbyterial charisms. On the other hand, I have discovered that people who have experienced this spiritual rebirth in their lives have been the most affirming of my ministry and have been very effective in convincing me of the special place the presbyterate has in the economy of the Church's life. The reality is: the more we call forth the gifts of Baptism, the more precious and effective the gift of Ordination becomes.

At the heart of the mission of the Church, then, is the Holy Spirit. This reality cannot be overemphasized. Let us hear what Pope Paul VI says in *Evangelii Nuntiandi*, the Decree on Evangelization in the Modern World:

> Evangelization will never be possible without the action of the Holy Spirit. The Spirit descends on Jesus of Nazareth at the moment of His baptism when the voice of the Father, 'This is my beloved Son with whom I am well pleased,' manifests in an external way the election of Jesus and His mission....It is in the power of the Spirit that He returns to Galilee and begins His preaching at Nazareth, applying to Himself the passage of Isaiah: 'The Spirit of the Lord is upon me.' And he

proclaims: 'Today this Scripture has been fulfilled.' To the disciples whom He was about to send forth He says, breathing on them, 'Receive the Holy Spirit'...

It is in "the consolation of the Holy Spirit" that the Church increases. The Holy Spirit is the soul of the Church. It is He who explains to the faithful the deep meaning of the teaching of Jesus and of His mystery. It is the Holy Spirit who, today just as at the beginning of the Church, acts in every evangelizer who allows himself to be possessed and led by Him. The Holy Spirit places on his lips the words which he could not find by himself, and at the same time the Holy Spirit predisposes the soul of the hearer to be open and receptive to the Good News and to the kingdom being proclaimed.

Techniques of evangelization are good, but even the most advanced ones could not replace the gentle action of the Spirit... It must be said that the Holy Spirit is the principal agent of evangelization; it is He who impels each individual to proclaim the Gospel, and it is He who in the depths of consciences causes the word of salvation to be understood (Par. 75).

What a powerful statement this is of the place of the Holy Spirit in the life and mission of the Church! He is our life; He is our strength; He is our inspiration; he is our success in every endeavor; He empowers our speech and he opens our ears to understanding; He releases our gifts and he prepares the groundwork for their use. Our whole being then should be immersed in the Holy Spirit. Our eternal prayer should be: "Come, O Holy Spirit, fill the hearts of the faithful. Enkindle in them the fire of your love."

If the Holy Spirit has such an important place in the life and mission of the Church, is this message getting through? For many it is. Today we are seeing people literally being transformed by the Holy Spirit and empowered to pursue ministries that were unthinkable for laity but a few decades ago. Many of the evangelists coming our way are laymen who have experienced life-changing conversions, have been baptized in the Holy Spirit, and are now powerful teachers and witnesses of the Gospel. A good example are the four men who teach and witness in our School of Evangelization. They are men who have been very successful in the world, did an about turn, and are now using their great talents to spread the Good News. As with the Apostles, they are witnesses of God's extraordinary power, changing their lives and compelling them to spend the rest of their lives in the service of the Lord. They are the fruit of Vatican Council II which called them forth, recognized their baptismal gifts, and empowered them in the Holy Spirit. Is it any wonder then that their message is so powerful and deeply touching for all who hear it?

I am firmly convinced that recognizing the place of the Holy Spirit in the Church and opening our hearts and minds to His transforming love is the most crucial and defining direction for the People of God today.

Yet there are examples in the Church where it seems that this priority is not at the heart of the evangelical thrust. The tragedy of defections, such as those in South America, should make abundantly clear to us the wisdom of the Council and Papal documents that highlight personal and communal transformation in the Holy Spirit, who is at the heart of Gospel and evangelical life. Our focus must be Jesus Christ, risen from the dead and living in His people personally and communally, liturgically, and sacramentally. Reflecting on this reality, Father Raymond Brown, eminent biblical scholar, has this to say:

> That Christ willed or founded the Church may be adequate theology for some; but an abstraction, focused on the past, will not be enough to keep others loyal to a Church unless they encounter Jesus there. They will join some small groups where they find an encounter with Jesus, even if these are tangential to or separated from the Church (*The Churches the Apostles Left Behind,* 97).

Today, I meet from time to time such people who have joined Evangelical churches to — in their words — be spiritually fed. This is always painful for me to hear and accept since I believe with all my heart that we have the fullness of spiritual riches in the Catholic Church if only we acknowledge it, take ownership of it, and proclaim it. These defected Catholics should meet our High School student mentioned above!

As we continue to reflect on the Church's call to evangelize, we might well reflect on these powerful documents — which many of our Separated Brethren seem to be implementing with greater fervor and force than we are — and allow them to give us a true focus for Gospel life and power once again. Not only will we bring new life to our own parishes, we will be offering the fullness of Gospel, sacramental, doctrinal, and communal life to the many who are hungering and yearning for salvation.

EIGHT

A Call to Pray for Peace
on Our Lenten Journey

As we approached the new millennium there was the threat of war looming for our country and for the world. Our Holy Father, Pope John Paul II, invited us to enter the Lenten Season that year in prayer and fasting for peace. In a pre-Lenten broadcast he stated:

> For months the international community has been living in great apprehension because of the danger of a war that might disturb the whole of the Middle East region and exacerbate the tensions that, unfortunately, are already present at the beginning of the millennium.
>
> It is a duty of believers, regardless of the religion to which they belong, to proclaim that we will never be able to be happy if we are against one another; the future of humanity will never be able to be assured by terrorism and the logic of war.
>
> We Christians, in particular, are called to be like guardians of peace in the places where we live and work. We are asked, that is, to be alert, so that

consciences will not yield to the temptation to egoism, falsehood and violence.

Because of this, our Holy Father invited "all Catholics to dedicate with special intensity on Ash Wednesday, to prayer and fasting for the cause of peace, especially in the Middle-East."

Our Holy Father went on to invite us to true conversion, which is the reason for the Lenten Season: "Above all, let us implore God for the conversion of hearts and a generous view in just decisions to resolve with adequate and peaceful means the contests that hamper the pilgrimage of humanity in our time."

During Lent we are to undertake penances as a loving expression of interior conversion. Acts of self-denial are an effort to detach ourselves from the attractions of the world, the flesh, and the devil. Purification of motive is an essential element that keeps our sights focused on the greater prize of union with God.

Our Holy Father reminded us of the value of fasting: "Christians share the ancient practice of fasting with many brothers and sisters of other religions, who in this way want to be despoiled of all pride and dispose themselves to receive from God the greatest and most necessary gifts, among which, in particular, is that of peace."

Since our Holy Father's message calls us to fasting, penance, and conversion, let us examine the connection between them. Acts of penance cannot be separated from internal conversion to the transforming power of God as it comes to us through Jesus in the Holy Spirit. *The Catechism of the Catholic Church* explains:

Jesus' call to conversion and penance, like that of the prophets before him, does not aim first at outward works, 'sackcloth and ashes,' fasting and mortification, but at the *conversion of the heart, interior conversion.* Without this spiritual transformation such penances remain sterile and false; however, interior conversion urges expression in visible signs, gestures and works of penance (1430).

Adult conversion is a deliberate decision, powered by grace, to renounce all allegiances that are not of God and to embrace the Lordship of Christ in everything that we are and do. It is the free and convincing surrender of our will to the will of our Father in Heaven in imitation of Jesus. "My food is to do the will of the one who sent me and to finish his work" (Jn. 4:34). Humble, obedient surrender to the divine will is at the heart of all worship. In the Book of Ecclesiastes we read: "Guard your step when you go to the house of God. Let your approach be obedience, rather than the fools' offering of sacrifice; for they know not how to keep from doing evil" (Eccl. 4:17). This theme is echoed in Psalm 40:7: "Sacrifice and offering you do not want; but ears open to obedience you gave me. Holocausts and sin-offerings you do not require." This verse would be applied to Jesus in the Letter to the Hebrews *(5:8-9)* to describe His mentality. Jesus clearly proclaimed that our relationship to Him is intimately connected with our obedient surrender to the will of His Heavenly Father:

But to the one who had told him this, Jesus replied, "Who is my mother, and who are my brothers?" And pointing to his disciples, he said, "Here are my mother and my brothers! For whoever does the will of my Father in heaven is my brother and sister and mother" (Mt. 12:48-50).

It is in obedience that Jesus reconciles humanity that was made destitute by disobedience: "For just as by the one man's disobedience the many were made sinners, so by the one man's obedience the many will be made righteous" (Rom. 5:8). It is in loving obedience to Christ and to his word that we find the rock on which to build our spiritual lives (Mt. 7:24). In St. John's Gospel we are assured that it is in this self-surrender to (belief in) Christ that we receive the fullness of life in the Holy Spirit.

On the last day of the festival, the great day, while Jesus was standing there, he cried out, "Let anyone who is thirsty come to me, and let the one who believes in me drink. As the scripture has said, 'Out of the believer's heart shall flow rivers of living water.'" Now he said this about the Spirit, which believers in him were to receive; for as yet there was no Spirit, because Jesus was not yet glorified (Jn. 7:37-39).

The call to holiness is a life-long journey that will be complete only when we embrace the Beatific Vision in Heaven and are perpetually absorbed in the Holy Trinity. What begins with Baptism continues in a day-to-day surrender that incorporates struggle and victory, failures and forgiveness, milestones, and new beginnings. *The Catechism* explains further:

> Interior repentance is a radical reorientation of our whole life, a return, a conversion to God with all our heart, an end to sin, a turning away from evil, with repugnance toward the evil actions we have committed. At the same time it entails the desire and resolution to change one's life, with hope in God's mercy and trust in the help of his grace. This conversion of heart is accomplished by a salutary pain and sadness which the Fathers called *animi cruciatus* (affliction of spirit) and *compunctio cordis* (repentance of heart) (1431).

We are offered the fullness of life, yet we struggle. We want the freedom of the Spirit, yet we are afraid to let go. We yearn for the power of God in our lives, yet we are reluctant to surrender control. We despise our helplessness, yet when the Holy Spirit rattles the cages of our comfort zones we retort and "kick against the goad" (Acts 26:14). This has been the struggle of the human heart from the very beginning. Jesus encountered it in his native Nazareth when he began his public ministry in the power of the Spirit (Lk.4:22ff). Throughout His public life, Jesus painfully experienced the lack of faith and stubborn blindness of His own people, which had its painful consequences in the past and would continue to close the doors to God's mercy and love now and in the future.

Yes, there is struggle today, but there is good news: The Holy Spirit is with us as our Comforter, our Consoler, our Advocate who pleads our cause. If we walk with him through life's desert, we will never be alone; we will never know discouragement. This is after all what makes the complete picture: a Lenten journey anointed and blessed by the Holy Spirit every step of the way.

In this time of peril let us pray that the fruits of the Spirit — love, joy, peace, patience, kindness, goodness, faithfulness, gentleness, self-control — will reign in our hearts and touch the hearts of all humanity. It is in the Spirit's love and consolation that we enter Lent's desert. It is in His sanctifying power that we die to self and experience the new life of Easter. A blessed dying and rising to all and may our ongoing prayer for peace profoundly influence the perilous future of world history.

NINE

The Riches of the Eucharist

Our Irish ancestors had a great devotion to the Mass. During Penal Times, which began in the sixteenth century under Henry VIII and ultimately repealed in Ireland in 1920, we saw Hell's fury come upon the Catholic Church in England and Ireland. As well as the confiscation of churches and properties, the destruction of monasteries, there was a price of five pounds on every priest turned over the authorities. Here is an example taken from the Government's records for 1657: "Five pounds to Rhoms Gregson, Evan Powell, and Samuel Ally, to be equally divided upon them, for arresting a Popish priest, Donoth Hagerty, taken and now secured in the County Gail at Clonmel." This is one of the edicts of the time:

> If anyone shall know where a priest remains concealed, in caves, woods, or caverns, or if by any chance he should meet a priest on the highway, and not immediately take him into custody and present him before the next magistrate, such person is to be considered a traitor and enemy of the Republic. He is accordingly to be cast into prison, flogged through the public streets and afterward have his ears cut off. But should it appear that he kept up any correspondence or friendship with a priest, he is to suffer death.

A Jesuit priest, in a report to his Superiors in Rome in the early sixteen fifties wrote:

> On a spot of ground in the middle of an immense bog, Father James Forde constructed for himself a little hut, to which boys and youths came and still come to be instructed in the rudiments of learning, virtue, and faith. Then they go from house to house and teach parents and neighbors that they learnt in the bogs.
>
> Our life is, therefore, a daily warfare and living martyrdom. We never venture to approach any houses of Catholics but live generally in the mountains, forests, and inaccessible bogs –where Cromwellian troops cannot reach us. Thither crowds of poor Catholics flock to us, whom we refresh with the Word of God and the Sacraments. Here in wild mountain tracts, we preach to them constancy in faith and the mystery of the Cross of Our Lord.

In spite of all precautions taken for the secret exercises, Cromwellians often discovered the hiding places. Then the wild beast was never hunted with more fury, nor tracked with more pertinacity, through mountains, woods, and bogs, than the priest.

"I cannot omit a lamentable incident which occurred here lately," says Father Quinn, "three hundred Catholics bound in chains, were carried to a desolate island–where they were abandoned. All of them starved to death except two who swam away. One sank. One reached the land" (c.f. McManus, *The Story of the Irish Race*, 434).

So we see why in Penal Times that poetry and prose were composed in allegory to hide their meaning from the enemy. In the Irish language, we have a beautiful example of this format in the song: "An Raibh Tu Ag An gCarraig?" ("Have you been to the Rock?) Have you seen my Love, the Eucharist?" Priests, who had a price on their heads, would gather at remote places with our ancestors to celebrate the Eucharist. This was their great consolation, in those dreadful times, to be able to unite their sufferings with those of Christ in this Mystery of Faith where His Passion, Death and glorious Resurrection were made present again. It was this faith in the Mass, together with the family Rosary, that sustained the faith in Ireland, and we are blessed and truly grateful today to be the beneficiaries of that faith and sacrifice.

The Mass is Word, Sacrifice, Sacrament, and Communion, which is the ultimate goal of all worship: being brought into intimacy with the Holy Trinity and the Heavenly hosts. In the Mass we first prepare ourselves with a communal act of sorrow seeking the Lord's forgiveness and purification for receiving the Word of God which "is living and active, sharper than any two-edged sword, piercing until it divides soul from spirit, joints from marrow; it is able to judge the thoughts and intentions of the heart" (Heb. 4:12). Essential to the call to holiness is the imbibing of and being true to the Word of God.

Throughout both Testaments, we see a common thread – the call to fidelity to the Word of God. When God's People were faithful to the Word they thrived. When they departed from it there was disaster and slavery. In the Old Testament, the Word was seen as something imposed from outside and difficult to endure. However, that was about to change with the coming of the Messiah as the prophet Jeremiah proclaimed: "But this is the covenant that I will make with the house of Israel after those days, says the Lord: I will put my law within them, and I will write it on their hearts; I will be their God, and they shall be my people" (Jer. 31:33). This is a prophecy of Pentecost. Somehow Jeremiah has already experienced Pentecost as we see him proclaim: "Your words were found, and I ate them, and your words became to me a joy and the delight of my heart; for I am called by your name, O Lord, God of hosts" (Jer. 15:16). Again the future Pentecost will be prophesied by Joel: "Then afterward I will pour out my Spirit on all flesh; your sons and your daughters shall prophesy, your old men shall dream dreams, and your young men shall see visions. Even on the male and female slaves, in those days, I will pour out my spirit" (Joel 2:28,29). Peter would quote this scripture on Pentecost Sunday. All of this will be fulfilled when Christ comes and through his redemptive action prepares his Church for the awesome riches that Word and Sacrament will release on his holy people.

The word "sacrifice" comes from the Latin *sacrificere*, meaning "to make holy." The word "holy" in turn means "set apart." We say that God is holy since His majesty is above and beyond all created beings. The Church is holy since, through the redeeming power of Christ, her members have been set apart by Baptism and have been adopted into the Family of the Holy Trinity. This reality is one that St. Paul proclaims in the Letter to the Romans: "Those who are led by the Spirit of God are children of God. For you did not receive a spirit of slavery to fall back into fear, but you received a spirit of adoption, through which we cry, 'Abba, Father!'" (8:14-15).

There is something inherent in our human nature calling us to give thanks for what we are and what we have received. When we receive a gift, we are truly grateful, but we are not at peace till we have sent a thank-you note or called to express our heartfelt gratitude. If this inherent need to give thanks is true in the human level – human to human, how much more is it intrinsic to the vertical level – the need to give thanks to God for his lavish generosity to us.

In our study of the human race, as far back as recorded history can lead us, we see evidence that our ancestors were deeply religious and were impelled to offer sacrifice to whatever they considered gods or the sources and sustenance of life. So, they worshipped the sun, the air, water, fire, and the earth. Their forms of worship included possessions most valuable to them, such as the first fruits of their flocks and harvest, or their precious metals. In many cultures, such as the Aztecs in Central America, they went so far as to offer their slaves, and even their children, in sacrifice to their gods. What was offered to the gods could no longer be used for any other purpose. So, the concept of immolation was adopted and the objects of sacrifice, whether human, animal, or plant, were burned. What the human spirit cried out was, "I want to offer my life in gratitude, and the only way I can do that is through what is of great value to me. This I will offer vicariously as a substitute for the giving of self."

St. Patrick came to Ireland in 432 A.D. and with the preaching of the Gospel and the anointing of the Holy Spirit the spiritual atmosphere and the form of worship would change dramatically. However, the holy bishop and his successors were prudent to take some of the former places of worship and give them a new form and meaning. For example, the Irish had made the spring water wells holy to them since drinking water was essential to their lives. St. Patrick would bless these wells so that now they would have a spiritual character and quality, where worship could take place and the waters be taken home for the blessing of family, animals, and crops. Where there were former places of worship such as mountains, islands, and other places of beauty, these too would be blessed and take on a Christian form. Two outstanding examples of pilgrimage associated with St. Patrick are Croagh Patrick in County Mayo and Lough Derg in County Donegal.

Croagh Patrick's history as a place of pilgrimage goes back over 5000 years and continues to the present day. Regarded as the holiest mountain in Ireland, it is still famous for its Patrician Pilgrimage in honor of St. Patrick. It was on the top of this mountain that St. Patrick fasted for forty days in the year 441 AD, and the custom continues faithfully, without interruption, from generation to generation to the present day. Its religious connection dates back to pagan times when it is believed that people gathered here to celebrate the beginning of the harvest season.

The other place of pilgrimage associated with St. Patrick is Loch Derg in County Donegal. It is known as St. Patrick's Purgatory and regarded as the most severe of penitential experiences. It involves three days of fasting and prayers while standing on sharpened rocks. It's not for everyone, but there must be a spiritual force that inspires people to return each year. Historically, the cave at St Patrick's Purgatory was considered a turnstile to the Gates of Hell, where in the fifth century St Patrick is said to have witnessed the tortures of eternal damnation. About 15,000 visitors come there every year. Not all, of course, take on the severe penitential experience.

So, where did the advance out of paganism, and the journey to faith really begin? About 2000 B.C. the true God began to reveal himself to Abraham and his descendants.

We learn in the Book of Genesis that Abraham left Ur, in Mesopotamia, because God called him to found a new nation in a new land, that he would later learn was Canaan. He obeyed unquestioningly the commands of God, from whom he received many promises and a sacred covenant guaranteeing that his "seed" would inherit the land. Human sacrifice will now be discontinued within the People of God, as we see in the story of the testing of Abraham. He was challenged to offer his son, Isaac, in sacrifice. As he was about to sacrifice his son, God gave Abraham a ram to offer instead (Gen. 22). What we have of course in this story is a foreshadowing of God the Father who will offer his only Son in sacrifice for our salvation. Jesus will now be the substitute for us and it is through his self-offering that satisfaction has been made for our sins.

Since sin is an offence against God, all of our offerings in atonement fall short. Only one who is on a par with God can make such an offering. That is why Jesus took on human nature so that as man he could die on our behalf. But it was as God that his offering had an infinite value. In the Letter to the Hebrews the author makes this very clear for us, as he contrasts the Old Testament sacrifices with that of Christ:

> When Christ came as high priest of the good things that were to come to be,...he entered once for all into the sanctuary, not with the blood of goats and calves but with his own blood, thus obtaining eternal redemption (c.f. Heb. 9:11ff).

What Jesus achieved through his passion, death, and resurrection, he now makes present again through the Sacrifice of the Mass. Here he invites us to hear his Word again as he proclaims it through the readers and celebrant. As we present the gifts of bread and wine, he invites us to offer ourselves with him to the Father in the power of the Holy Spirit. This self-offering leads to inner transformation as we die to the old self of sin and attractions and distractions that drag us away from God.

This transformation is expressed in the elements we offer. Bread has its origin in the grain of wheat that goes down into the ground and dies. In dying it gives life to many grains of wheat, which in turn are ground into flour and through the miracle of baking become a new substance — bread. Similarly, the grapes, pressed into juice and through the miracle of fermentation, become a new substance — wine. This process of natural transformation now prepares these elements for another transformation into the Body and Blood of Christ at the consecration.

This process of transformation now applies to us. At Baptism, we become a new creation. We are, as we mentioned above, adopted into the life of the Holy Trinity. As we come of age, we are as children taught to make our morning offering. In doing so we are asking the Lord to bless our day with its work, its joys, its sorrows, its sacrifices, etc., so that everything we do may be to the glory of God, for our salvation and the salvation of the world. However, it is when we come to Mass that this offering of self finds its perfect transformation. As the gifts of bread and wine are offered, we are invited to offer ourselves. As the elements are transformed on the altar, we also experience ongoing transformation. We die to the old ways of the flesh and enter more deeply into the ways of the spirit. St. Gregory of Nazianzen said, and I paraphrase: "Of what value is it for me to make Jesus present on the altar if I do not die with him so as to rise with him."

It is this self-offering that allows us to enter the Paschal Mystery. We die with Jesus so that we may rise with him. Now when we receive Our Savior in Holy Communion we are more open to his transforming love and are more intimately assimilated into the divine. St. Paul says, "I have been crucified with Christ; yet I live, no longer I, but Christ lives in me" (Gal. 2:20). Again: "We know that our old self was crucified with him, so that our sinful body may be done away with, that we might no longer be in slavery to sin…Consequently, you must think of yourself as being dead to sin and living for God in Christ Jesus" (Rom. 6:6ff).

Thomas à Kempis, in his classic, *The Imitation of Christ*, put these words on Christ's lips:

> Look, I offer myself wholly to the Father for you; I also gave my whole body and blood for you for food, that I might be wholly yours, and you should remain mine. But if you stand upon yourself and do not offer yourself freely to my will, the offering is not fully made nor will union between us be complete.

Therefore, let us respond with Thomas à Kempis:

> Lord, all things are yours in heaven and on earth. I long to offer myself to you for a freewill offering, and to remain forever yours. Lord, in the sincerity of my heart, I offer myself to you today to serve forever, for obedience and for a sacrifice of unending praise. Receive me with this holy offering of your precious Body, which today I offer you, in the presence of the Angels, invisibly around, that it may be for salvation for me and for all people (Imitation of Christ IV, 8).

Finally, it is the Holy Spirit who reveals to us the mysteries of our faith in all of their riches and transforming power. So, we pray:

Come, Holy Spirit, forth from the Heart of Christ, and enflame our hearts and minds with that interior light so that we can grasp the height and the depth of the mysteries of our faith, be transformed by them, and generously share their riches, especially with those who are in darkness and in the shadow of death, Amen. Let us prepare then each day for a fuller participation in the Mass, which is "the source and summit of the Christian life" (Vatican Council II).

Again, let us keep in mind that we are not capable of perfect self-giving on our own. That is the work of the Holy Spirit. If it was in the power of the Holy Spirit that Jesus offered himself to the Father (Heb. 9:14), surely our self-offering, to be efficacious, must be patterned on that of our Savior.

Here are some quotes from the Saints on the power and beauty of the Eucharist:

O King of glory, though you hide your beauty, yet the eye of my soul rends the veil. I see the angelic choirs giving you honor without cease....All the good that is in me is due to Holy Communion. I owe everything to it. I feel this holy fire has transformed me completely....In all my sufferings and struggles, I was not omitting Holy Communion....Jesus, source of my life, sanctify me. O my strength, fortify me. My commander, fight for me....Holy Communion assures me that I will win the victory; and so it is. I fear the day when I do not receive Holy Communion. The bread of the Strong gives me all the strength I need to carry on my mission and to do whatever the Lord asks of me....The mercy of God, hidden in the Blessed Sacrament, the voice of the Lord who speaks to us from the throne of mercy: Come to me, all you who labor....You left us Yourself in the Sacrament of the Altar, and you opened wide your mercy to us. There is no misery that could exhaust You; You have called us all to this fountain of love, to this spring of God's compassion. – St. Faustina

O Christ, let my greatest delight be to see You loved and Your praise and glory proclaimed, especially the honor of Your mercy. O Christ, let me glorify Your goodness and mercy to the last moment of my life, with every drop of my blood and every beat of my heart. Would that I be transformed into a hymn of adoration of You. When I find myself on my deathbed, may the last beat of my heart be a loving hymn glorifying Your unfathomable mercy. Amen. – St. Faustina

If we but paused for a moment to consider attentively what takes place in this Sacrament, I am sure that the thought of Christ's love for us would transform the coldness of our hearts into a fire of love and gratitude. – St. Angela of Foligno

Christ held Himself in His hands when He gave His Body to His disciples saying: 'This is My Body.' No one partakes of this Flesh before he has adored it. Recognize in this bread what hung on the cross, and in this chalice what flowed from His side... whatever was in many and varied ways announced beforehand in the sacrifices of the Old Testament pertains to this one sacrifice which is revealed in the New Testament. – St. Augustine

Lord, we cannot go to the pool of Siloam to which you sent the blind man. But we have the chalice of Your Precious Blood, filled with life and light. The purer we are, the more we receive. – St. Ephraim

When the bee has gathered the dew of heaven and the earth's sweetest nectar from the flowers, it turns it into honey, then hastens to its hive. In the same way, the priest, having taken from the altar the Son of God (who is as the dew from heaven, and true son of Mary, flower of our humanity), gives him to you as delicious food. When you have received Him, stir up your heart to do Him homage; speak to Him about your spiritual life, gazing upon Him in your soul where He is present for your happiness; welcome Him as warmly as possible, and behave outwardly in such a way that your actions may give proof to all of His Presence. – St. Francis de Sales

What wonderful majesty! What stupendous condescension! O sublime humility! That the Lord of the whole universe, God and the Son of God, should humble Himself like this under the form of a little bread, for our salvation...In this world, I cannot see the Most High Son of God with my own eyes, except for His Most Holy Body and Blood. – St. Francis of Assisi

Do grant, oh my God, that when my lips approach Yours to kiss You, I may taste the gall that was given to You; when my shoulders lean against Yours, make me feel Your scourging; when my flesh is united with Yours, in the Holy Eucharist, make me feel Your passion; when my head comes near Yours, make me feel Your thorns; when my heart is close to Yours, make me feel Your spear."– St. Gemma Galgani

I hunger for the bread of God, the flesh of Jesus Christ ... I long to drink of his blood, the gift of unending love. – St. Ignatius of Antioch

Jesus taught a new sacrifice which the Church received from the Apostles and offers throughout the whole world. – St. Irenaeus

If Christ did not want to dismiss the Jews without food in the desert for fear that they would collapse on the way, it was to teach us that it is dangerous to try to get to heaven without the Bread of Heaven. – St. Jerome

Do you realize that Jesus is there in the tabernacle expressly for you – for you alone? He burns with the desire to come into your heart...don't listen to the demon, laugh at him, and go without fear to receive the Jesus of peace and love. Receive Communion often, very often...there you have the sole remedy, if you want to be cured. Jesus has not put this attraction in your heart for nothing. The guest of our soul knows our misery; He comes to find an empty tent within us – that is all He asks...How I loved the feasts! I especially loved the processions in honor of the Blessed Sacrament. What a joy it was for me to throw flowers beneath the feet of God!... I was never so happy as when I saw my roses touch the sacred Monstrance. – St. Therese of Lisieux

"Rabbi, where are you staying?" Each day the Church responds: Christ is present in the Eucharist, in the sacrament of His death and resurrection. In and through the Eucharist, you acknowledge the dwelling-place of the Living God in human history. For the Eucharist is the Sacrament of the Love which conquers death. It is the Sacrament of the Covenant, pure Gift of Love for the reconciliation of all humanity. It is the gift of the Real Presence of Jesus The Redeemer, in the bread which is His Body given up for us, in the wine which is His

Blood poured out for all. Thanks to the Eucharist, constantly renewed among all peoples of the world, Christ continues to build His Church: He brings us together in praise and thanksgiving for salvation, in the communion which only infinite love can forge. Our worldwide gathering now takes on its fullest meaning, through the celebration of the Mass. Dear young friends, may your presence here mean a true commitment in faith! For Christ is now answering your own question and the questions of all those who seek the Living God. He answers by offering an invitation: This is My Body, take It and eat. To the Father He entrusts His supreme desire: that all those whom He loves may be one in the same communion. – From St. John Paul II's World Youth Day homily on Sunday, August 24, 1997, in Paris, France

From St. Thomas Aquinas, great theologian and poet of the Eucharist, we share the following:

Because last words, chiefly such as are spoken by departing friends, are committed most deeply to memory; since then especially affection for friends is more enkindled, and the things which affect us most are impressed the deepest in the soul. Consequently, since, as Pope Alexander I says, "among sacrifices, there can be none greater than the body and blood of Christ, nor any more powerful oblation"; our Lord instituted this sacrament at His last parting with His disciples, in order that it might be held in greater veneration.

St. Thomas Aquinas composed the liturgy for Corpus Christi when Pope Urban IV added the Solemnity to the universal Church's liturgical calendar in 1264. So, the Church has been enriched with the beautiful poetry and depth of theology that these masterpieces have passed on to us:*Victimae Paschali Laudes* (Christians, To the Paschal Victim) for Easter Sunday; *Veni Sancte Spiritus* (Come, Holy Spirit) for Pentecost, and *Lauda Sion Salvatorem* (Sion, praise the Savior). For Benediction: *O Salutaris and Tantum Ergo.*

This is one of my favorite hymns of St. Thomas that I have loved to share:

Adore te, devote, latens Deitas; I adore you devoutly, hidden Deity,

Quae sub his figuris verelatitas; truly hidden under these symbols.

Tibi se cor meum totus subicit; I totally submit my heart to him,

Quia te contemplans, totum deficit; because in contemplating you I am totally deficient.

Visus, tactus, gustus in te fallitur; Sight, touch, taste are deceived in you,

Sed auditu solo tute creditur; But in hearing only, are you safely believed.

Credo quidquid dixit Dei Filius; I believe whatever the Son of God says,

Nil hoc verbo veritatis verius; Nothing is true if his word is not true.

God dwells in our midst, in the Blessed Sacrament of the altar... He remains among us until the end of time.... The culmination of the Mass is not the consecration, but Communion...You come to me and unite Yourself intimately to me under the form of nourishment. Your Blood now runs in mine, Your Soul, Incarnate God, compenetrates mine, giving courage and support. What miracles! Who would have ever imagined such!....If angels could be jealous of men, they would be so for one reason: Holy Communion...God dwells in our midst, in the Blessed Sacrament of the altar. – St. Maximilian Kolbe

Here are some testimonies of persons who have been deeply touched when the power of the Holy Spirit releases the spiritual riches of Christ in His Word and Sacrament:
May 1999

Dear Father:
The following is the shortened version of the many extraordinary blessings which the Lord has poured out upon me in the last few weeks, since the start of the Life in the Spirit Seminar.
Before the introductory session, I felt an overwhelmingly powerful mandate not to attend the seminar. I was plagued with doubts and irrational fears, discouragement, feelings of worthlessness,

and very strong feelings of rejection. These feelings continued to bombard my spirit day and night. I felt that my whole being was being pushed down to the ground. I felt very weak and depressed. To combat what I was feeling, I fasted on bread and water and read Scripture, attending the Perpetual Adoration Chapel whenever I was able.

I've had many encounters with the enemy, most of which I have handled on my own, with very little spiritual direction. This is not because I did not seek the direction, but because there are many leaders in the Church who are ignorant of the pervasive presence of the enemy in our world today. One priest told me that it was impossible that the enemy was attacking our family because we were "too Catholic!" As the mother of eight children, God has armed me with a knowledge of the enemy's tactics, some of which I have attained through reading and some of which I have learned through direct experience.

One of the ways that the enemy exposes his otherwise subtle and sneaky attempts to stunt my spiritual growth is that when I do not cooperate with his plans, he steps up this assault. The patience that I have in suffering is what causes him to overdo his attack and he is thus revealed to me. Then I was undergoing the feelings of futility and rejection. I was not sure if they were based in reality or were unfounded fears. It was the enemy's frantic suggestions that I was disliked by everyone at St. Veronica's, etc. that unveiled this presence to me.

His desperation that I was not giving in to his prompting was his undoing.

And so, I stubbornly dragged myself to the first session of the Seminar, still experiencing the feelings, but refusing to let them know what was going on in my head. At the meeting, my spirit was lifted up. I thought that the battle was over. But as soon as I left the meeting. I was plunged down into the depths once again. I felt that I could not go back. I continued to pray that I would have the courage to return the following week. God answered my prayer, and that is when everything started to happen.

The first sign that a healing was in progress took place during the second week of the Seminars. During the meeting which was held in St. Veronica's School Library, I felt that my spirit was being opened up, though there was great reluctance on my part. After the meeting ended, I felt compelled to go to the Perpetual Adoration Chapel. While I was there, I was concentrating very intently on the Real Presence of Jesus in the Monstrance. I have great powers of concentration and when I am in deep prayer, I do not often notice things that are happening around me. I was vaguely aware that adorers were coming and going during this time. Suddenly, I became aware that I knew, without a shred of doubt, that you, Father, were present in the Chapel. I do not know how I knew this, but I was absolutely positive about your presence there. Simultaneous with this knowledge, I felt in the fingertips of my left hand a tingling and a certain heat accompanied by a surge of power which slowly emanated through my hand, up my arm, and radiated through my neck and the left side of my face. The vibration and the heat landed on three definite spots on my brain. It felt like the opposite motion of a drill, like the undoing of a migraine headache.

Whereas a migraine feels like a pain which is boring a hole in your brain, this sensation felt like a drill was going in the opposite direction, like it was releasing pressure in three definite spots. As I have said, I knew, without a doubt, that you, Father, were in the Chapel. But I felt that I could not move my head to look because I felt like I was definitely experiencing the healing power of God and that wherever you were, it was coming through you. I don't know how I knew this, but I was positive about this. I thought that perhaps my former migraine headaches were being healed, although it had been a few years since I had suffered from one. After an unspecified period of time, I turned my head to the left and I was surprised to see you kneeling right beside my chair with your right hand resting on the arm of the chair. My left hand was barely touching the arm of the chair. You left momentarily and I felt the effects of the healing power for the rest of the hour or so that I remained. I believe that what was healed that night was not only a certain hurtful memory of my childhood but also the release of a person whom I thought I had forgiven long ago. The way it happened was that as the spots on my brain were pulsating, I had a vision of my mother, which I quickly pushed away. It was like I was saying to Jesus that I could not deal with thinking about her right then. Then, I saw my grandmother. I remember thinking, "Oh, this is ridiculous. I forgave Grandma long ago for the abuse that she put me through." And this is true. I had gone through a psychodrama with a licensed psychologist, in which I played out the parts of myself and my grandmother and put to rest the memories of the past abuses. But, as I was thinking about this, I felt this middle spot on my brain drilling deeper and pulsating wildly. It was like I was being told not to discard this thought. And so, I gave the Spirit free reign to roam the corridors of my mind, and to control the situation. I let go and just watched like I was in a theatre watching a play in which I was one of the actors. What resulted was that the memory was viewed by me in a totally different way than at previous times. The Spirit showed me a new perspective on my grandmother's actions, one which I had never even considered. What I had always done was to play out the memory and then be a martyr and tell Grandma that I forgave her for her terrible actions toward me. But now I was being shown the real reasons that she acted the way she did, which were very different from what I had previously comprehended. The tears began to flow as I realized that this memory was really being healed, not just being covered over by a mental Band-Aid. There was much love, understanding, and pity extended to my grandmother through Jesus, the Bridge of our separate worlds. Whereas before, when I would think about the past hurts, it was as if she was out there in Eternity and I was here in the Present, and the memory was the connection; now, I felt as if I had been taken to her to hold her hand and to tell her that I understood why she did what she did and that I truly forgave her. It was beautiful; it was serene; it was God in my pitiful world showing me that nothing is impossible with Him. Father, there are two more "brain spots" that continue to vibrate whenever you come into the Chapel. I suppose that I cannot yield to the Spirit to heal these memories. My conscious mind wants to be healed, but perhaps my subconscious mind is not letting go. I believe that I know that they involve my mother and my husband and that they are most likely related to forgiveness. However, I have not been able to experience the complete healing of these memories. I am not sure how to proceed. I want to be free to invite the Spirit into my life without reservation. I also wanted to relate to you an experience of being set free from addiction after the Tuesday evening Healing Mass in April. But time does not permit me to go into it at this time, and I know that your schedule must be unbelievably busy. Please pray for me as I do for you constantly. I am so grateful to God for leading our family to St. Veronica's and to you, Father.

May God continue to bless you. Yours in Christ, – C.

Another person offers the following testimony:

First Letter: April 9, 1996

Greetings:
I wanted to take this moment to thank you for all you have done to welcome me into St. Veronica's parish community. Our meeting on the Monday of Holy Week helped me to focus on how important the power of Jesus can be in my life. I came to the Easter Vigil with a peaceful and open heart, knowing that my life will only be better with God and the Holy Spirit in it.

I savor the moments of my Baptism, Confirmation, and finally the Eucharist, that I will treasure forever. You made the evening very special for my husband Tom and I, and we both wanted you to know it. I am looking forward to learning and growing even more through the Life in the Spirit Seminar and the Healing Masses in the months to come. Thanks again for being so caring. Sincerely, – L.

Second letter: June 4, 1999
I have been moved to write about your recent article in the Sunday Bulletin. Your words about the Holy Spirit always encourage me to seek more spiritual awareness in my own life.

During my darkest times, you taught me to pray to Our Father and to accept his will. By turning my life over to God, I in effect became the infant in St. Matthew's Gospel, and my life has changed dramatically.

I have enclosed a quote that was printed in the Bulletin on the Fourth Sunday of Lent, written by me in the Adoration Chapel. It sums up, in a few words, our pain of losing four children, and the joy of receiving our son, Daniel.

I believe that by prayer and by complete submission to the will of God, my prayers to keep the child alive were answered. Through Daniel I see the Holy Spirit shining on me every day. I know that all parents feel their children are special, but I believe that Daniel is our miracle from God. The pain of losing four children still haunts my heart, but our Daniel came to us when it seemed hope was futile.

I am overwhelmed each day by the loving nearness of God. I encounter through my individual act of faith through prayer the intimacy of the Holy Trinity. In the three years since my Baptism, I have seen God work over and over again in my life. I am living proof that the Gospel works and is for real. As always, your remarks and writings have moved me to consider God's place in my life. God bless you, Father. – L.

May all of these reflections and testimonies help us grow in our love and appreciation of Christ in the Eucharist.

TEN

The Rosary: Its Power; Its Miracles

Our Catholic tradition tells us that through Saint Dominic and Blessed Alan de Rupe the Blessed Virgin Mary made fifteen specific promises to Christians who pray the Rosary. The fifteen stated promises range from protection from misfortune to meriting a high degree of glory in heaven. Here are those promises:

Whoever shall faithfully serve me by the recitation of the rosary shall receive signal graces.

I promise my special protection and the greatest graces to all those who shall recite the rosary.

The rosary shall be a powerful armor against hell; it will destroy vice, decrease sin, and defeat heresies.

It will cause virtue and good works to flourish; it will obtain for souls the abundant mercy of God; it will withdraw the heart of men from the love of the world and its vanities, and will lift them to the desire of eternal things. Oh, that souls would sanctify themselves by this means.

The soul which recommends itself to me by the recitation of the rosary shall not perish.

Whoever shall recite the rosary devoutly, applying himself to the consideration of its sacred mysteries, shall never be conquered by misfortune. God will not chastise him in His justice, he shall not perish by an unprovided death; if he be just he shall remain in the grace of God, and become worthy of eternal life.

Whoever shall have a true devotion for the rosary shall not die without the sacraments of the Church.

Those who are faithful to recite the rosary shall have, during their life and at their death, the light of God and the plenitude of His graces; at the moment of death they shall participate in the merits of the saints in paradise.

I shall deliver from purgatory those who have been devoted to the rosary.

The faithful children of the rosary shall merit a high degree of glory in heaven.

You shall obtain all you ask of me by the recitation of the rosary.

All those who propagate the holy rosary shall be aided by me in their necessities.

I have obtained from my Divine Son that all the advocates of the rosary shall have for intercessors the entire celestial court during their life and at the hour of death.

All who recite the rosary are my sons, and brothers of my only son Jesus Christ.

Devotion of my rosary is a great sign of predestination.

Our Lady gave the Rosary and these accompanying promises to the Church for all of her children, literate and illiterate, so that all could be equally blessed and enriched in the recitation of this powerful prayer. The history of this great prayer has had many astonishing results in the lives of the faithful and on the course of history itself.

September 12, 1213 was the day of the Battle of Muret, when Count Simon de Montfort (father of the founder of the English parliament) and 700 knights had defeated the Albigensian army of some 50,000. While the battle raged, St. Dominic and his friars were praying the Rosary in the church of Muret.

On October 7th, 1571 a fleet of ships assembled by the combined forces of Naples, Sardinia, Venice, the Papacy, Genoa, Savoy and the Knights Hospitallers, fought an intense sea battle with the fleet of the Ottoman Empire. The battle took place in the Gulf of Patras located in western Greece. Though outnumbered by the awesome fleet of the Ottoman forces, the so-called "Holy League" possessed a superior power that came from Heaven that would win the day. This victory would severely curtail attempts by the Ottoman Empire to control the Mediterranean, causing a major shift in international relations from East to West. We can say perhaps with certainty today that the West was saved from Muslim domination by this extraordinary victory. The victory at the Battle of Lepanto will forever be associated with the Holy Rosary.

It was Pope Pius V, himself a gift from the Order of St. Dominic, who, from the Vatican Treasury, helped finance the military endeavor. He would now call upon the faithful to unleash power from the spiritual treasury. He ordered the churches of Rome to be opened for prayer day and night, encouraging the faithful to petition the intercession of the Blessed Virgin Mary through the recitation of the Rosary. On the day of the sea battle, October 7, 1571, the Holy Father joined with a group of the faithful in Rome at the Dominican Church and prayed the

Rosary. At the end of the recitation of the Rosary, we are told that the Pope received an inner message that the Catholic fleet had crushed the Ottomans.

When the victory of the Holy League was hailed publicly in Rome, the Pope added a new feast day to the Roman Liturgical Calendar. October 7th would henceforth be the feast of Our Lady of Victory. Pope Pius' successor, Gregory XIII, would change the name of this day to the feast of the Holy Rosary. Today, the name with which we commemorate the victory's feast day, October 7th, is Our Lady of the Rosary.

Another detail from the armada: Admiral Andrea Doria, commander of the Catholic forces, carried an image of Our Lady of Guadalupe into battle. This image is now venerated in the Church of St. Stefano in Aveto, Italy.

On September 11, 1683 came the Battle of Vienna. King Jan (John) III Sobieski of Poland-Lithuania had entrusted his kingdom to the protection of our Lady of Czestochowa before the battle. His forces were also bolstered by Christendom-wide praying of the Rosary. With the divine and earthly powers united, his forces delivered Vienna and Christendom once again from the Muslim Ottoman Turks whose army was numbered at about 500,000. The Holy Roman Empire of Emperor of Leopold I was saved from imminent destruction, thanks again to Our Lady and her Rosary.

For three years, Catholic Austria went under the tyrannical rule of Communist Russia after World War II. A Franciscan priest named Father Petrus remembered the story of the Rosary's victory at Lepanto in 1571. So he launched a Rosary Crusade and 70,000 Austrians pledged

25

to pray the Rosary for Austria's liberation from the Russians. Austria was important to the Communists because of its location in Europe and its wealth of resources. Yet, on May 13th, the anniversary of the first apparition in Fatima, the communist Russian regime, in what was a completely unexpected and unexplained move, signed an agreement to leave Austria. To this day historians and military experts are at a total loss as to the reason why the Russians left Austria.

During World War II, on August 6, 1945, a devastating event occurred. An atom bomb was dropped on Hiroshima, Japan. The destruction was astronomical. The death toll was 140,000. There was a church about eight blocks from the site of the bomb explosion. The church was completelydestroyed. Yet, extraordinarily, the attached rectory survived with the eight priests within, who were German Jesuits missionaries. These men prayed the Rosary daily in that rectory. The reason that they were still living and working in Hiroshima was due to the fact that Germany and Japan were allies during the war. Yet these priests suffered no radiation, hearing loss, or any other form of disease or major injury. This was verified by several medical tests later. When they were asked what was it that saved them, they would reply that they were living the message of Fatima. "We lived and prayed the Rosary daily in that rectory."

On May 13, 1984, one of the largest crowds in Fatima history gathered to pray the Rosary for peace. That same day, an explosion at a Soviet naval base destroyed an estimated two-thirds of all the missiles stockpiled for the

Soviets' Northern Fleet. Again, thanks to you, Our Lady of the Rosary.

And finally, we cannot forget the extraordinary way in which Central and Eastern Europe were delivered from the evil grasp of Communism without firing a shot. Here the powerful leadership of Pope John Paul II demonstrated once again the presence of Our Lady. As a child he consecrated himself to Our Lady following the inspiration of St. Louis de Montfort's classic, *True Devotion to Mary.* The future Pope would take *Totus Tuus,* Totally Yours, as his motto. This defines his determination to have entrusted his life, his priesthood and his papacy, yes, everything to Mary. He explains:

This phrase is not only an expression of piety, or simply an expression of devotion. It is more. During the Second World War, while I was employed as a factory worker, I came to be attracted to Marian devotion. At first, it had seemed to me that I should distance myself a bit from the Marian devotion of my childhood, in order to focus more on Christ. Thanks to St. Louis de Montfort, I came to understand that true devotion to the Mother of God is actually Christocentric; indeed, it is very profoundly rooted in the Mystery of the Blessed Trinity and the mysteries of the Incarnation and Redemption.

I will add here a personal experience I had while in Lourdes. After our devotions at the Grotto, I returned to my hotel room. Suddenly I received a clear interior message: "Return to the Grotto now and pray the Rosary for a specific named Cleric." I did as I was instructed and did not think of the experience again. However, after my return home, I learned that this person had a miraculous healing. Our Lady's Rosary triumphed once again.

Here are some quotes from the saints on their love and admiration of Mary the Mother of Jesus:

> We never give more honor to Jesus than when we honor his Mother, and we honor her simply and solely to honor him all the more perfectly. We go to her only as a way leading to the goal we seek – Jesus, her Son. The greatest saints, those richest in grace and virtue will be the most assiduous in praying to the most Blessed Virgin, looking up to her as the perfect model to imitate and as a powerful helper to assist them. – St. Louis Marie de Montfort

> Mary having cooperated in our redemption with so much glory to God and so much love for us, Our Lord ordained that no one shall obtain salvation except through her intercession. – St. Alphonsus Maria de Liguori

> Men do not fear a powerful hostile army as the powers of hell fear the name and protection of Mary. – St. Bonaventure

> To give worthy praise to the Lord's mercy, we unite ourselves with Your Immaculate Mother, for then our hymn will be more pleasing to You, because She is chosen from among men and angels. Through Her, as through a pure crystal, Your mercy

was passed on to us. Through Her, man became pleasing to God; Through Her, streams of grace flowed down upon us. – St. Faustina

Never be afraid of loving the Blessed Virgin too much. You can never love her more than Jesus did. – St. Maximilian Kolbe

In dangers, in doubts, in difficulties, think of Mary, call upon Mary. Let not her name depart from your lips, never suffer it to leave your heart. And that you may obtain the assistance of her prayer, neglect not to walk in her footsteps. With her for a guide, you shall never go astray; while invoking her, you shall never lose heart; so long as she is in your mind, you are safe from deception; while she holds your hand, you cannot fall; under her protection you have nothing to fear; if she walks before you, you shall not grow weary; if she shows you favor, you shall reach the goal. – Saint Bernard of Clairvaux, Father and Doctor of the Church

O sinner, be not discouraged, but have recourse to Mary in all your necessities. Call her to your assistance, for such is the divine Will that she should help in every kind of necessity. – Saint Basil theGreat

Mary, give me your Heart: so beautiful, so pure, so immaculate; your Heart so full of love and humility that I may be able to receive Jesus in the

Bread of Life and love Him as you love Him and serve Him in the distressing guise of the poor. – St. Teresa of Calcutta

If you invoke the Blessed Virgin when you are tempted, she will come at once to your help, and Satan will leave you. – St. John Vianney

When we were little, we kept close to our mother in a dark alley or if dogs barked at us. Now, when we feel temptations of the flesh, we should run to the side of our Mother in Heaven, by realizing how she is to us, and by means of aspirations. She will defend us and lead us to the light. – St. Josemaria Escriva

There are many other beautiful quotes from the saints available on the internet.

In this reflection on our Blessed Mother, I am brought back to childhood and the family Rosary; the May Altar when we gathered the beautiful wild spring flowers to honor her; the Legion of Mary in our Grade School; singing the Marian hymns with my sister, Helen (now St. Mary Brenda) in our parish choir throughout the year at Our Lady's feasts. How beautiful, warm, comforting, and secure it was to be her beloved children.

ELEVEN

The Call of the Church to Evangelize

Now the eleven disciples went to Galilee, to the mountain to which Jesus had directed them. When they saw him, they worshiped him; but some doubted. And Jesus came and said to them, "All authority in heaven and on earth has been given to me. Go therefore and make disciples of all nations, baptizing them in the name of the Father and of the Son and of the Holy Spirit, and teaching them to obey everything that I have commanded you. And remember, I am with you always, to the end of the age" (Mt.28:16-20).

It seems that evangelization has become a natural outgrowth of charismatic renewal. From what we can read from the actions of the Holy Spirit in the church in the 20th century, the ground was being prepared for what our Holy Father John Paul II then called a springtime of evangelization in the Church. With the Vatican II documents and the writings of subsequent popes, it was clear that the place of the Holy Spirit in the Church has been brought very much to the fore. Pope John Paul II summed it up well in his encyclical *The Splendor of Truth* as he emphasized the central role of the Holy Spirit in the ministry of evangelization:

At the heart of the new evangelization and the new moral life which it proposes and awakens by its fruits of holiness and missionary zeal, there is the Spirit of Christ, the principle and strength of Holy Mother Church.

Pope Saint Paul VI reminds us in these words: "Evangelization will never be possible without the Holy Spirit."…As Novatian once pointed out – here expressing the authentic teaching of the Church – it is the Holy Spirit "who confirmed the hearts and minds of the disciples, who revealed the mysteries of the Gospel, who shed upon them the light of things divine. Strengthened by his gift, they did not fear either prisons of chains for the name of the Lord; indeed they even trampled upon the powers and torments of the world, armed and strengthened by him, having in themselves the gifts which this same Spirit bestows and directs like jewels to the Church, the Bride of Christ. It is in fact he who raises up prophets in the Church, instructs teachers, guides tongues, works wonders and healings, accomplishes miracles, grants the discernment of spirits, assigns governance, inspires counsels, distributes and harmonizes every other charismatic gift. In this way he completes and perfects the Lord's Church everywhere and in all things (154).

Cardinal Ratzinger, who later became Pope Benedict XVI, reflecting on the 'new Pentecost,' called our time a "Pentecostal hour."

The period following the Council scarcely seemed to live up to the hopes of Pope John XXIII, who looked for a "new Pentecost." But his prayer did not go unheard. In the heart of a world, desiccated by rationalistic skepticism, a new experience of the Holy Spirit has come about, amounting to a worldwide renewal movement. What the New Testament describes, with reference to the charisms, as visible signs of the coming of the Spirit is no longer merely ancient, past history: This history is becoming a burning reality today (Ratzinger Report, 151).

The new thrust toward evangelization is indeed quite new for Catholics. Our experience has shown us that many people in the Church are suspect of Catholic lay evangelists and do not quite know how to accept them at first. When they experience the power of the Holy Spirit working through them in their witness, their transformed lives and their solid Catholic teaching, they are overjoyed that at last the Catholic Church is entering a field that seems till now has been populated by Protestant evangelicals. Father Avery Dulles reflects:

> The majority of Catholics are not strongly inclined toward evangelization. The very term has for them a Protestant ring. The Catholic Church is highly institutional, sacramental, and hierarchical in its structures. Its activities are primarily directed toward the institution and pastoral care of its own members, whose needs and demands tax the

institution to its limits. Absorbed in the inner problems of the Church, and occasionally in issues of peace and justice, contemporary Catholics feel relatively little responsibility for spreading the faith (*John Paul II and the New Evangelization*, 3).

However, Father Dulles tracks a significant change in the Church's focus since Vatican II:

> In my judgment the evangelical turn in the ecclesial vision of Popes Paul VI and John Paul II is one of the most surprising and important developments in the Catholic Church since Vatican II...For them, as for the kerygmatic theologians, the heart and center of evangelization is the proclamation of God's saving love and shown forth in Jesus Christ. Where the name of Jesus is not spoken there can be no evangelization in the true sense... All of this constitutes a remarkable shift in the Catholic tradition. For centuries evangelization was a poor step-child....Today we seem to be experiencing the birth of a new Catholicism, that without loss of its institutional, sacramental, and social dimensions, is authentically evangelical...Catholic spirituality at its best has always promoted a deep personal relationship with Christ...Too many Catholics of our day seem never to have encountered Christ. They know a certain amount about him from the teaching of the Church, but they lack direct personal familiarity...The first and highest priority is for the Church to proclaim

the good news concerning Jesus Christ as a joyful message to all the world, only if the Church is faithful to its evangelical mission can it hope to make its distinctive contribution in the social, political and cultural spheres" (ibid., 13, 16-17).

Let us continue to pray that this "new Pentecost" will continue to take hold in the Church and enkindle a fire of evangelization that will bring about a glorious harvest of souls for Christ throughout the world.

"Like good stewards of the manifold grace of God, serve one another with whatever gift each of you has received. Whoever speaks must do so as one speaking the very words of God; whoever serves must do so with the strength that God supplies, so that God may be glorified in all things through Jesus Christ. To him belong the glory and the power forever and ever. Amen" (1 Peter 4:10-11).

The focus of our preaching and teaching then is conversion to Christ as our personal Lord and Savior. This conversion comes about through the anointing of the Holy Spirit who leads us to an intimate experience of Jesus Risen and glorified, and releases gifts for inner transformation and holiness, and for ministry to the Body of Christ and the proclamation of the Gospel to the world.

Evangelization in Dublin

The summer of 1996 brought us on a new adventure in evangelization as the team from Good News International and I set out for Dublin, Ireland to conduct our first School in the Emerald Isle. In March I had returned to my native land to preach the Youth Conference in Cork and the positive experience there was a great confidence builder for me to answer another call in the service of the Gospel.

My sister, Sr. Mary B., had done all the organizational work for the School to begin on Sunday, July 7th at St. Patrick's Training College in Drumcondra, which is across the street from All Hallows College where I was ordained. We flew out from Newark on July 4th in an atmosphere of joy and excitement as we looked forward to what would be a historic week in Dublin. When we settled in at St. Patrick's we had time for prayer, relaxation, and a trip downtown to the legendary city that has been acclaimed over the centuries by her literary and artistic sons and daughters. With Pat Egan, a native Dubliner, and myself as guides, our group received a courier's introduction to the history and topography of the Fair City.

On Saturday we traveled to the Midlands to visit friends in County Offaly. Since we were close by, we decided to go to Clonfert, the site of St. Brendan's famous sixth century monastery. In recent years a spiritual center has been established there with a beautiful circular chapel that captures a sense of the past in its architecture and art. We arrived there at three in the afternoon and the staff and visitors were delighted to learn that a priest was available for Mass. As we began our prayer with the Divine Mercy chaplet, I could not help but wonder if our being at Clonfertwas not indeed part of God's plan to usher in a new age of evangelization in Ireland. It was here that St. Brendan established one of Ireland's greatest schools. His own navigational exploits for the spread of the Gospel are legendary and are handed down to us in *Navigatio*

Brendani, which was widely circulated in the whole of Europe throughout the Middle Ages. It is possible that Brendan reached the coast of Florida, judging by his descriptions of a land luxuriant with fruits and flowers. One exploration scholar, Tim Severin, convinced that Brendan was writing about real navigational experiences, decided to construct a boat to the exact specifications found in *Navigatio* and successfully sailed across the Atlantic to North America in 1976 (*The Brendan Voyage*, 1978). In 1492 Columbus sailed to Galway to research the records and traditions of Brendan. This visit, together with the names of Irishmen on the roster of the Santa Maria on the voyage to America, is recorded in the National Archives of Madrid.

We are told that the communities of Brendan reached about 3000 monks who looked to him for inspiration and guidance. This was undoubtedly a splendid charismatic age in the Irish Church. The Gospel was preached with power and was accompanied by many miracles. The very name Clonfert in ancient Irish, *Cluan Fearta*, means Field of Miracles. In these monasteries spirituality and learning went hand in hand. Students from Europe came in great members to this sanctuary of spirituality and civilization to bring back to their homes what had been lost in the Dark Ages. A flood of missionaries went out to establish monasteries and universities so that the light of reason, blessed by the light of faith, might begin a new day in the life of a devastated Continent.

Church historian, Daniel-Rops, on reflecting on this age, calls it "The Irish Miracle" which he said is "the second setting out of Christianity, from a country which had just been baptized, and was immediately dreaming of giving Christ back to the world. Ireland, between the 5th and the 8th century, was like a second Palestine, a new cradle of the Christian faith."*(The Saints of Ireland, ix).*

As we celebrated Mass in this restored Spiritual Center, I marveled at how appropriate it was to begin our week of evangelization here. I sensed the presence of my patron and all the holy men and women of the age of saints and scholars gather round the altar to invoke the Holy Spirit's anointing on our Gospel venture. The same Spirit who sent forth a torrent of light from Ireland to the world was now bringing back the recipients of that light to help renew the Irish Church.

After sharing the hospitality of the wonderful people at the Center we went on to Clonmacnoise, another famed seat of spirituality and learning which also was given birth in the sixth century, under the direction of St. Kieran. Of this the Irish bard O'Gillan (finely translated by Rollaston) would write:

In a quiet watered land, a land of roses, stands St. Kieran's city fair;

And the warriors of Erin in their famous generations, slumber there.

Together with Clonfert, this "city fair", with its famous Scripture crosses and round towers, would for centuries educate Europe's students and serve as an artery of scholars and evangelists to Europe and beyond. As I sat amid these hallowed ruins on this pleasant summer day I prayed that our team of seven would be blessed and anointed as Kevin's seven were when they arrived at Clonmacnoise on a cold January day in 545 A.D. to begin their awesome mission. This visit afforded us some very precious moments to bathe in the light and imbibe in the spirit of another charismatic age in the life of the Church. It was a good feeling to share such a noble mission with the great men of ages past. Slowly I rose to meander toward the exit. As I gazed at the great Scripture cross for the last time before we began our return journey to Dublin, the words of Longfellow's *Psalm of Life* began to scroll across my consciousness:

Lives of great men all remind us, we must make our lives sublime;

And in departing leave behind us, footprints on the sands of time.

We were ready now to begin our first School of Evangelization in Ireland.

At St. Patrick's Training College sixty-five enthusiastic participants from many parts of Ireland were ready for the week's encounter. Cardinal Daly, Primate of All Ireland, wrote a most encouraging letter of welcome to us and sent his blessing to all the participants. When Sr. Mary B. read it to the group, it was received with great joy and somehow set the tone for the week that this was an event not just of a small group but indeed an experience that connected the whole Irish Church.

The response was wonderful and the Holy Spirit was present in a very powerful way. Judging from the letters we have received since we returned, it was an intensely spiritual experience for all. Here is a letter from a couple from County Leitrim, which reflects the spirit of other mail we received:

I just had to write to you to thank you for the wonderful five days we had with you and your team of men who came to Dublin. It was the most blessed week of our married life. I felt so close to God through all of you and especially on the night of our anniversary. I had felt from the first moment I heard of the school of evangelization that it would be a lovely way to celebrate our anniversary. But it completely surpassed any dream I had. We experienced a beautiful healing in so many ways throughout the five days. I also feel that it is only the beginning as we got so much that we have food for thought and spiritual growth for a long time to come.

This letter confirmed for us the need for evangelical outreach to the spiritual hunger and brokenness that still is imbedded in the hearts of our brothers and sisters in the Church. We are also reminded of the sincere gratitude that is expressed when these spiritual needs are met. This brings to mind one of my favorite quotes from St. Bonaventure regarding the process of the spiritual journey of the soul to God:

In this passing over, if it is to be perfect, all intellectual activities ought to be relinquished and the loftiest affection transported to God, and transformed into Him. This, however, is mystical and most secret, which no one knows except him who receives it, and no one receives it except him who desires it, and no one desires it except him who is penetrated to the marrow by the fire of the Holy Spirit, Whom Christ sent into the world. That is why the Apostle says that this mystical wisdom is revealed by the Holy Spirit (The Journey of the Mind to God, 38).

Though it came from just one source, we also experienced intense anger that was directed toward the Church. We never like to encounter such negative forces, yet it was nonetheless a blessed opportunity for us to really deal with hurt and anger, and move toward reconciliation, forgiveness and healing. The recent problems in the Church in Ireland have only intensified what is endemic to every community — hurt, bitterness, rage, rejection, antagonism, jealousy, resentment. Our school was very sensitive to these realities and carefully ministers to them. What could have been a disaster for the unprepared turned out to be a great moment of deep healing and liberating spiritual renewal. At the heart of conversion to the Church is the painful yet indispensable process of repenting of our sins against the Church and forgiving the Church for all the hurts we have received from those who represent the Church. We offered that moment of healing grace when I stood before the group and in the name of the Church asked those gathered for forgiveness.

Some of our team members who have been in the ministry for several years said that this was the most intense and powerful week that they had ever experienced. Without a doubt, we were all spiritually and emotionally renewed by the Dublin experience and returned glorifying

God that He had visited the Irish Church and had used us as His instruments.

My sister, Sr. Mary B., had organized a spirituality day for the group in Dublin in October to continue the spirit of the week and plan for future ventures for the spread of the Gospel. Already a School of Evangelization was being planned for July 1997 in Cork. Our constant prayer was that the Good News would continue to spread throughout the Church. Our School of Evangelization was open to and encouraged all of the spiritual and charismatic gifts. We believed that these gifts were given to be used for personal sanctification and for the spread of the Gospel. It is clear that when the Irish Church was a powerhouse of evangelization, it was blessed with saints who were powerful preachers, great scholars, and miracle workers, driven by the Spirit, as Jesus was, to bring the Gospel to every creature.

During our schools we would pray for the outpouring of the Holy Spirit on all present. We explained the charismatic gifts and encouraged an openness to the full complement of gifts that were bestowed in our Baptism and Confirmation. We explained that many of our gifts lay dormant until we consciously surrender to the Holy Spirit for their awakening. The degree to which we are open to and take ownership of our baptismal gifts will determine the degree of fruitfulness we will enjoy in celebrating the other sacraments and in living out our Christian vocation. This is why we see Baptism in the Holy Spirit as crucial to the renewal of the Church and to the spread of the Gospel in our times. We encouraged forgiveness of the Church for all the hurts we have received from those who represented the Church. We offered that moment of healing grace when I stood before the group and in the name of the Church asked them for forgiveness.

The Irish Bishops in their 1993 pastoral on Catholic Charismatic Renewal have recognized the wonderful blessings it has brought to the Church:

> The Irish Bishops have seen many fruits of the Charismatic Renewal during the past twenty years. Thousands have found deeper commitment to Christ, a deep love for the Holy Scriptures, an openness to the gifts of the Holy Spirit, profound gifts of prayer including spontaneous prayer, greater understanding of the Eucharist and of the Church, a fruitful love of their brothers and sisters.

They go on to strongly endorse the Life in the Spirit Seminars:

> These (seminars) prepare people to open their hearts to God, to turn from sin, to embrace the cross in daily life, to hope for the transforming power of the Holy Spirit. These seminars have been for millions throughout the world a most graced means of bringing people into the conversion experience of the Outpouring of the Holy Spirit. They have been used for conversion and evangelization even outside the Charismatic Renewal.

It was most gratifying to learn that the Irish Bishops had already endorsed just about everything our School represented and desired to achieve. As servants of the

Church in the mission of evangelization we will continue to answer the Holy Spirit's call, under the guidance and direction of the Magisterium, to spread the Good News that Jesus Christ is Lord. We were indeed following the mission of the Apostles and of all the saints, scholars, and evangelists that have followed them. St. Patrick's Breastplate was a powerful prayer, protecting and energizing our ministry through the week.

> I arise today through a mighty strength, the invocation of the Trinity, Through belief in the Threeness, Through confession of the Oneness of the Creator of creation. I arise today through the strength of Christ's birth with His baptism, Through the strength of His crucifixion with His burial, Through the strength of His resurrection with His ascension, Through the strength of His descent for the judgment of doom.
>
> I arise today through the strength of the love of cherubim, in the obedience of angels, in the service of archangels, in the hope of resurrection to meet with reward, in the prayers of patriarchs, in the predictions of prophets, in the preaching of apostles, in the faith of confessors, in the innocence of holy virgins, in the deeds of righteous men.
>
> I arise today, through The strength of heaven, The light of the sun, The radiance of the moon, the splendor of fire, The speed of lightning, The swiftness of wind, The depth of the sea, The stability of the earth, The firmness of rock.

I arise today, through God's strength to pilot me, God's might to uphold me, God's wisdom to guide me, God's eye to look before me, God's ear to hear me, God's word to speak for me, God's hand to guard me, God's shield to protect me, God's host to save me From snares of devils, From temptation of vices, From everyone who shall wish me ill, afar and near. I summon today All these powers between me and those evils, Against every cruel and merciless power that may oppose my body and soul, Against incantations of false prophets, Against black laws of pagandom, Against false laws of heretics, Against craft of idolatry, Against spells of witches and smiths and wizards, Against every knowledge that corrupts man's body and soul; Christ to shield me today Against poison, against burning, Against drowning, against wounding, So that there may come to me an abundance of reward. Christ with me, Christ before me, Christ behind me, Christ in me, Christ beneath me, Christ above me, Christ on my right, Christ on my left, Christ when I lie down, Christ when I sit down, Christ when I arise, Christ in the heart of every man who thinks of me, Christ in the mouth of everyone who speaks of me, Christ in every eye that sees me, Christ in every ear that hears me. Amen.

TWELVE

The Mass and Adoration:
Its Power; Its Miracles

Hundreds of thousands of people of all ages and backgrounds come to daily Mass and Jesus is always waiting for them; waiting to feed them on His Word and Sacrament. He continually descends onto the altar waiting to sacrifice Himself so He can come to life in them and transform them. But it is not enough to be present at Mass and receive Jesus' Eucharistic body. As Church we have a universal call to holiness; to deepen our interior life and union with Christ.

Caryll Houselander, British mystic and teacher tells us, "Jesus becomes a living active Presence in our lives if we open ourselves and allow Him." Yes, if we allow Him is the key.

Saint John of the Cross writes:

> God dwells secretly in all souls…yet there is a difference, a great difference in His dwelling in them. In some He dwells alone, in others He is not alone. Abiding in some He is pleased; in others He is displeased. He lives in some as though in His own house; in others He is like a stranger in a

strange house, where they do not permit Him to do anything.

It is important for us to believe that Jesus desires to come into our heart. He desires to celebrate the Eucharist and waits for us to receive Holy Communion. St. John Paul II said, "In Holy Communion we do not receive Jesus as much as He receives us. He accepts us as we are; He receives, accepts and loves us." Yes, God comes to us as love; He not only wants to be with us but to be inside of us at every moment.

Are we longing to meet Christ in His Word and Sacrament in the Holy Mass? Do we prepare for the miracle on the altar? Do we hunger for Jesus coming in the form of bread and wine to purify and transform us? We must be watching, waiting in vigil for the coming of the Lord into the deserts of our hearts. He, the Lord of all creation, wants to unite Himself with us. Yes, Christ wants to put Himself in our hands; He allows us to adore Him in the palms of our hands. He pours over them rivers of graces. Yet, He loves us and respects our freedom; He permits us to make use of the graces or reject them.

When I receive Him in Holy Communion, He allows me to hold Him and adore Him in the palm of my hands. It is at this time that I kiss our Eucharistic Lord in the host, express my love, and ask forgiveness for the wounds that I and my family have caused Him.

Scott Hahn in *The Lamb's Supper* states:

> We receive Him, whom we praised in the Gloria and proclaimed in the Creed! In the

Eucharist we receive what we will be for all eternity, when we are taken up to heaven to join with the heavenly throng in the marriage supper of the Lamb. When Christ comes at the end of time, He will not have one drop more glory than He has at the moment, when we consume Him. At Holy Communion, we are already there.

The greater our faith and love, the more effective the Eucharist will become in our lives....The growth in faith will enable us to discover the real presence of Jesus and to discover the making present of His redemptive sacrifice. We will begin to know Him even better, who He is and what happens on the altar. To quote Father Tadeusz Dajczer,

> The Eucharist is still the undiscovered land, the unknown world. Your God wants to introduce you to his stunning truth that is regularly occurring on our altars." We must be alert that our participation in Mass and receiving Holy Communion not become routine. We should try to participate in the Mass as if it were the first or last Mass of our lives. We should prepare ourselves with holy longing and awaiting Him. We are so blessed to do all things through Mother Mary and with Mary. She can keep us close and faithful to our Eucharistic Lord.

St. Louis Marie de Montfort advises us to "invite Mother Mary to participate in the Mass and Eucharist with us." When we ask Mary to stand between us and Christ, we become closer to Him. In our love for Him, we want her hands and lips, which are the only ones worthy, to touch His Body and caress His wounds.

Testimony on the Power of Eucharistic Adoration

As a child in Catholic elementary school I preferred to visit Jesus in Church in front of the tabernacle rather than join others on the playground. I knew He was there in the tabernacle, but I didn't realize He wanted to be with me also. Later in high school, Jesus drew me closer to Him in the Eucharist. Again, the most precious hours were with Him before the Blessed Sacrament during times spent with the religious community at the high school.

As the years of adulthood passed, the Lord continued to bless me in the Holy Mass or in Eucharistic Adoration with His love. These blessings occurred most often when on silent retreats with Him, during or after Mass. My earliest experience occurred during my first Charismatic Conference at a Catholic University. I decided to attend Exposition of the Blessed Sacrament and Adoration. A special room had been set aside, and as I entered I noticed it was almost filled to capacity. I chose to kneel in the back behind all the chairs. Immediately upon kneeling I was pulled forward as if by a giant magnet; I was not strong enough to resist this pull and my body was drawn to lie prostrate on the ground. Spontaneously, praise and words of love poured out of me for our Eucharistic Lord.

I remained prostrate in prayer for an extended period of time, how long I do not know. Adorers began to leave and only a few remained, so I managed to move up to the front, closer to Jesus in the Monstrance. Again, I was drawn by the powerful pull to lie prostrate and time disappeared. Jesus was present and showed me the horrific abuse and shame He suffered at the hands of the guards. I wept as He looked at me and I sensed Him say, "I did this for you so your burden of pain and shame would be less." I thanked Him in a river of tears and promised Him I would pray for victims all my life.

At midnight on Christmas Eve 1997 I went to Eucharistic adoration to be with Jesus and sing carols to Him in the silence of my heart. Only a few people were there as I entered the sacred space in holy silence. Our Eucharistic Lord was present in the Monstrance, waiting and thirsting for those He loves to come and be with Him. Joy overflowed as I sat in silence with Him. At some point in time the other people left and I am alone with the Alone. As I gazed on the Sacred Host, I no longer saw the Host; rather I saw the Infant Jesus. I doubted myself and attributed it to my imagination. The Infant Jesus remains until the time of my departure. I still attribute all to my imagination.

A week or two later a parishioner and Eucharistic Adorer whom I do not know comes up to me at Church and asks if I am [name]. I responded, "Yes, I am." She replies, "While in prayer with the Lord, He asked me to find you and to let you know it was Him, the Infant Jesus, in the Monstrance with you on Christmas Eve." I weep in thanksgiving for so precious a gift!

One morning I left the house early to attend 6:30 a.m. daily Mass at the local Church. The Church is on the way to the school where I teach. This has been my daily pattern for years and allows enough time for Mass and to arrive at work by 7:30 a.m. Arriving at school this particular morning, I experienced the sacred Host that I received at Mass resurfacing intact in my mouth. I was unsure of what was happening, for it had never occurred before. Wanting to enter the building and go immediately to my private office to pray, I encountered the opposite. One of my young freshman students was encircled by a group of older, angry upperclassmen ready to fight. Without hesitation I walked into the center of the circle and said clearly, "Robert, come upstairs with me I need your help." He stayed close and followed me up the stairs. When we arrived upstairs, I let him stay in the classroom, and I went into my office to consume the Host and give thanks to the Lord for this precious gift. I know it was the Lord's Eucharistic Presence within me that permeated the whole situation downstairs with His peace.

On retreat in March 1998, during morning prayer, I read 1 Samuel 10:9: "As Saul turned to leave Samuel, God gave him another heart." In Mass that morning I asked the Lord to pierce my heart open and make it new, so that it will never close on any of His children. In response, I sensed Him say, "Your new heart will be a heart of flesh, very vulnerable and easily wounded. It will feel all."

Later, I would sense being physically emptied and then filled with His presence, as stated in Psalm 81: "Open wide your mouth and I will fill it." During afternoon adoration I began to sense Jesus drawing out my breath and into Him in the Monstrance. Simultaneously, I sensed a beam of His light from His heart piercing my big stony heart and breaking it into pieces. It continued as I surrendered all to Him. He gave me a new heart and asked me to love Him in everyone He brings into my life. "Your vocation is love, my child. Wipe my face, help me carry my cross, run to greet me in morning prayer, love me with the first love you had for me."

Retreats in silence and solitude with the Lord continued for many years. Throughout those years the Lord continued to reveal Himself and draw me closer to Him in the Mass or in Eucharistic Adoration. Thankfully, our rich Church tradition provides us with many wise and Holy guides for prayer as listed below.

"We must be watching, waiting in vigil for the coming of the Lord in the desert of our hearts. Silent, solitary prayer is needed to nurture a spirit of recollection." – Desert Father, Eugene Romano – Bethlehem Hermitage

"We must be put in a divine silence. Not a silence coming from men, but a silence that comes from God." – Blessed Elizabeth of the Trinity.

In February of 2002 in adoration, I placed the relic of the True Cross over my heart and rested in Jesus' arms. Earlier I had asked Jesus to take me deeper into Him, to break open my heart in His Mercy, to transform and transfigure me. Jesus answered my prayer. What transpired and seemed like 15 minutes, lasted over one hour.

The sun coming into the room penetrated through the relic of the cross and into me. It became one beam of light. I saw my heart and soul as lava trapped in a layer of crust that forms when hot lava reaches cool water. I asked Jesus by the power and light of His cross to break open the crust on my heart and soul and let the fire of love stream out. He heard my prayer.

The light flowed out of the Cross on my chest, and my heart and soul opened wider and wider. Boundaries and edges of my body disappeared. I was without boundaries in a consuming fire, in Jesus's heart and soul and He in me. Tears flowed and I prayed spontaneously. Tears of joy took me deeper into Him; tears of joy that He was residing in me and filling me. I asked Him, "What should I do? Should I go to the Tabernacle in the chapel?"

He answered me by expanding out further in this lava of love, this consuming fire. We expanded out across the grounds and over the chapel. There His Eucharistic Presence in the Host entered my heart at the center of this flow of love. I wept at the union. I knew the Father, Jesus the Holy Spirit, and I were one edgeless, consuming fire of love. I opened my eyes and I could not see the wooden ceiling, only light blue expanse, emptiness. Then, the whitest purifying light appeared from the left. I wept again and prayed in the Spirit for purification. It seemed like wisps of clouds were streaming toward the white light, souls I believed. I prayed, "Jesus I trust in You."

Afterwards, my body slowly regained form, and contracted around my soul. I experienced my soul having dominion over my body. I didn't know what to do and decided to go to Jesus in the Blessed Sacrament although He filled me already. I walked across the grounds and moved very slowly and prayed, "Lord protect me from any experience that is not of You." I asked Jesus and Mother Mary to show me what to do since they experienced this in prayer. I asked the Lord to lead me to a priest for spiritual direction.

In May of 2006, during our 20 minute contemplation after Holy Communion, I was filled with the flesh and blood of Christ. His light was first, then His precious blood traveling into the parts of my body. Suddenly the Host inside of me expanded and expanded. My arms went out wide to hold the edges of the Sacred Host; I was in the Host and the Host was in me. Jesus asked me to be His Monstrance for all the world to see.

My reaction: like Mary at the Annunciation – "How can this be Lord? I am not worthy." I sensed Him say, "Just let me take you into My heart and don't worry. I want you in My heart."

The following morning immediately after receiving Christ's Body and Blood in Holy Communion, I felt an explosion of Jesus' Presence within. My body, this earthen vessel could not contain my Lord. Every part of my body was filled to capacity, could not expand anymore with His Presence. I could feel our hearts beating as one. After Mass, I asked the holy priest about this because I was worried it might happen in public. His response to me was, "I have experienced this many times, just surrender to the Lord, His love is too great to contain."

Later that day, I returned from Vespers and read Carroll Stuhlmueller's writings on the "Transfiguration." He writes:

We as a temple of God are where the Father, Son, and Holy Spirit have come to make their dwelling place. The glory which will transform us when we share in the Resurrection of Jesus already resides at the core of our existence. Here dwells

Jesus, one with the Father and the Spirit, in this inner Holy of Holies. We already possess what we will be; transfiguring our lives now in small but significant ways.

Occasionally its inspirations and insights, its secret hopes and joys break through and transfigure, at least momentarily. These are wonderful and awesome moments when God summons us to leap beyond all earthly limitations and with our earthly body to perform heroic deeds. These moments of visions can frighten us, so great is the joy of expectation. We can and should seek spiritual advice. The ultimate decision is ours alone with God.

I pray that these writings will enlighten, inspire and increase our yearnings for our Eucharistic Lord.

We thank you so very much for this testimony!

The Eucharist is the living Heart of Christ truly present, Body, Blood, Soul, and Divinity, that has been our awesome blessing in the Church since the Last Supper. Through the centuries it has been the spiritual Food of our great saints and our humble peasants. Belief in the Real Presence has been initiated, bolstered, and intensified by the Holy Spirit. We have encountered this reality time and time again in our ministry through the years. The love of the Mass, Word, Sacrament, and the attraction to Eucharistic Adoration have been clear signs of the working of the Holy Spirit. We have seen this growth in faith blossom in all who have experienced the Life in the Spirit Seminars. With St. Paul they can cry out: "It is no longer I who live, but it is Christ who lives in me. And the life I now live in the flesh I live by faith in the Son of God, who loved me and gave himself for me" (Gal. 2:20).

Sadly, today, we are experiencing in the Catholic Church a severe drop in faith in the Real Presence. A recent survey by the Pew Research Center claims that up to seventy percent of Catholics do not believe that Jesus is really present in the Eucharist. Pretty shocking indeed. We hope it will help if we offer the case of two miracles of the Eucharist.

In 1995 I was invited to an International Conference on Healing which took place at San Giovanni Rotondo, the home of St. Pio of Pietrelcina. The conference featured Father Emiliano Tardif whose personal story was quite an amazing one. A native of Quebec, he fell ill with pulmonary tuberculosis in June 1973. He had to go back home to Canada from the Dominic Republic to be urgently hospitalized at the Tuberculosis Hospital in Quebec. Following several medical tests doctors told him that maybe after one year of treatment, he might be able to leave the hospital. While in the hospital, he received a visit from five lay people from a Charismatic Prayer group in Quebec. They prayed with him and after a few days he was completely healed.

Following his healing, he began to study the Catholic Charismatic Renewal and attended Retreats and Conferences so as to know more about this new Pentecost that the Lord was bringing to the Catholic Church. He received the charism of healing in November 1973. Back in the Dominican Republic, he proceeded to preach and use his great gift of healing in five continents. It was indeed a great privilege to have him at the Conference, absorb his great preaching and receive his healing blessing. He went home to the Lord in June 1999, leaving behind years of powerful preaching and miraculous hearings throughout the world. His cause is now up for canonization. While at the Conference, it was also a singular blessing for me to celebrate Mass at the tomb of St. Pio. Since that time it has been discovered that his body was incorrupt and is now open for veneration.

On Saturday of the week of the Conference a group of us drove to Lanciano, where the eighth century miracle of the Eucharist took place. Again it was a blessed honor to have the opportunity of celebrating Mass in front of the Ostensorium that contains the Eucharistic Miracle.

Briefly, here is the story of this extraordinary event: A Basilian priest, who had lost his faith in the Real Presence, grieved at this loss and prayed for help to believe. An extraordinary miracle took place as he was celebrating Mass. After the two-fold consecration, the host was changed into live Flesh and the wine was changed into live Blood, which coagulated into five globules, irregular and differing in shape and size. The Host-Flesh, as can be very distinctly observed today, has the same dimensions as the large host used today in the Latin church; it is light brown and appears rose-colored when illuminated from the back. The Blood is coagulated and has an earthy color resembling yellow ochre. Various ecclesiastical investigations have been conducted since 1574.

In 1970-71, and taken up again partly in 1981, there took place a scientific investigation by the most illustrious scientist Prof. Odoardo Linoli, eminent Professor in Anatomy and Pathological Histology and in Chemistry and Clinical Microscopy. He was assisted by Prof. Ruggero Bertelli of the University of Siena. The analyses were conducted with absolute and unquestionable scientific precision and they were documented with a series of microscopic photographs.These analyses led to the following conclusions:

The Flesh is real Flesh. The Blood is real Blood. The Flesh and Blood belong to the human species. The Flesh consists of the muscular tissue of the heart. In the Flesh we see present in section: the myocardium, the endocardium, the vagus nerve and also the left ventricle of the heart for the large thickness of the myocardium. The Flesh is a "heart" complete in its essential structure. The Flesh and Blood have the same blood-type: AB (Blood-type identical to that which Prof. Baima Bollone uncovered in the Holy Shroud of Turin). In the Blood there were found proteins in the same normal proportions (percentage-wise) as are found in the sero-proteic make-up of the fresh normal blood. In the Blood there were also found these minerals: chlorides, phosphorus, magnesium, potassium, sodium and calcium.

The preservation of the Flesh and Blood, which were left in their natural state for twelve centuries and exposed to the action of atmospheric and biological agents, remains an extraordinary phenomenon.

Yes, it was a special honor for me to have had the opportunity to celebrate Mass in the presence of this extraordinary mystery.

The second miracle in our story comes from Buenos Aires:

In 1996 in the Archdiocese of Buenos Aires, Argentina, when Pope Francis was Auxiliary Bishop under Cardinal Quarracino, an amazing Eucharistic miracle took place. He himself had it photographed and investigated and the results are astonishing.

The facts of what took place are narrated by Ron Tesoriero in his book *Reason to Believe,* published in 2007.

On August 18, 1996 Fr. Alejandro Pezetwas celebrating Mass at a Catholic church in the commercial center of Buenos Aires. As he was finishing distributing Holy Communion, a woman came up to tell him that she had found a discarded host on a candle holder at the back of the church. On going to the spot indicated, Fr. Alejandro saw the defiled Host. Since he was unable to consume it, he placed it in a container of water and put it away in the tabernacle of the chapel of the Blessed Sacrament. On Monday, August 26, upon opening the tabernacle, he saw to his amazement that the Host had turned into a bloody substance. He informed Bishop Jorge Bergoglio (Now Pope Francis, Auxiliary Bishop at that time), who gave instructions that the Host be professionally photographed. The photos were taken on September 6. They clearly show that the Host, which had become a fragment of bloodied flesh, had grown significantly in size. For several years the Host remained in the tabernacle, the whole affair being kept a strict secret. Since the Host suffered no visible decomposition, Cardinal Bergoglio (who became Archbishop by that time) decided to have it scientifically analyzed.

On October 5, 1999, in the presence of the Cardinal's representatives, Dr. Castanon took a sample of the bloody fragment and sent it to New York for analysis. Since he did not wish to prejudice the study, he purposely did not inform the team of scientists of its provenance (the source of sample was kept secret to the scientists). One of these scientists was Dr. Frederic Zugibe, the well-known cardiologist and forensic pathologist and former Medical Examiner of Rockland County. He determined that the analyzed substance was real flesh and blood containing human DNA. Zugibe testified that the analyzed material is a fragment of the heart muscle found in the wall of the left ventricle close to the valves. This muscle is responsible for the contraction of the heart. It should be borne in mind that the left cardiac ventricle pumps blood to all parts of the body. The heart muscle is in an inflammatory condition and contains a large number of white blood cells. This indicates that the heart was alive at the time the sample was taken since white blood cells die outside a living organism. They require a living organism to sustain them. Thus, their presence indicates that the heart was alive when the sample was taken. What is more, these white blood cells had penetrated the tissue, which further indicates that the heart had been under severe stress, as if the owner had been beaten severely about the chest.

Two Australians, journalist Mike Willesee and lawyer Ron Tesoriero, witnessed these tests. Knowing where the sample had come from, they were dumbfounded by Dr.

Zugibe's testimony. Mike Willesee asked the scientist how long the white blood cells would have remained alive if they had come from a piece of human tissue, which had been kept in water. Dr. Zugibe replied that they would have ceased to exist in a matter of minutes. The journalist then told the doctor that the source of the sample had first been kept in ordinary water for a month and then for another three years in a container of distilled water; only then had the sample been taken for analysis. Dr. Zugibe was at a loss to account for this fact. There was no way of explaining it scientifically. Also, Dr. Zugibe passionately asked, "You have to explain one thing to me, if this sample came from a person who was dead, then how could it be that as I was examining it the cells of the sample were moving and beating? If this heart comes from someone who died in 1996, how can it still be alive?"

Only then did Mike Willesee inform Dr. Zugibe that the analyzed sample came from a consecrated Host (white, unleavened bread) that had mysteriously turned into bloody human flesh. Amazed by this information, Dr. Zugibe replied, "How and why a consecrated Host would change its character and become living human flesh and blood will remain an inexplicable mystery to science; a mystery totally beyond her competence."

Then Doctor Ricardo Castanon Gomez arranged to have the lab reports from the Buenos Aires miracle compared to the lab reports from the Lanciano miracle, again without revealing the origin of the test samples. The experts making the comparison concluded that the two lab reports must have originated from test samples obtained from the same person. They further reported that both samples revealed an AB positive blood type. They are all characteristic of a man who was born and lived in the Middle East region.

Only faith in the extraordinary action of a God provides the reasonable answer: faith in a God, who wants to make us aware that He is truly present in the mystery of the Eucharist. The Eucharistic miracle in Buenos Aires is an extraordinary sign attested to by science. Through it Jesus desires to arouse in us a lively faith in His real presence in the Eucharist. He reminds us that His presence is real, and not symbolic. Only with the eyes of faith do we see Him under appearance of the consecrated bread and wine. We do not see Him with our bodily eyes, since He is present in His glorified humanity. In the Eucharist Jesus sees and loves us and desires to save us.

There is also proof of the extraordinary power of Christ's Real Presence in the Eucharist: the saints and mystics who lived on the Eucharist alone for years. Here are just a few of those saints and blessed souls who lived on the Eucharist alone for long periods of time:

St. Catherine of Siena lived on the Eucharist alone for the last seven years of her life. Her family and friends tried to get her to eat some natural food. However, it made her sick, and they discontinued their efforts. St. Catherine also had the stigmata, the miraculous wounds of Christ. She asked the Lord to make them invisible during her lifetime. He acceded and the wounds became visible only after her death.

St. Catherine of Genoa lived on the Eucharist alone during her fast times at Advent and Lent.

St. Joseph Cupertino lived on the Eucharist alone for five years.

St. Anne Catherine Emmerich, we are told, had the use of reason from birth and understood Latin from the first time that she attended Mass. During the last twelve years of her life she lived on the Holy Eucharist alone and could drink only water. She also had the stigmata of Jesus during her remaining years on earth.

One of the most well-documented cases in modern times is that of Blessed Alexandrina da Costa who lived on the Eucharist alone for thirteen years. During this time, she took neither food or drink. She is regarded as the fourth seer of Fatima. She went home to the Lord in 1955. Her cause for canonization is now in progress.

We also have the extraordinary account of Marthe Robin who lived on the Eucharist alone for 51 years. Born in France in 1902, by 1928 Marthe's lower body was paralyzed; by 1929 so were her arms. Marthe was living at home in a dark bedroom due to her hypersensitivity to light. By the age of 28, she was completely paralyzed and bedridden. Early on she still could use her thumb and forefinger and was able to finger her rosary beads. Eventually she lost the ability to do even that. All she could do was move her head. She could no longer eat or even take a sip of water. Doctors tried to force water down but it would come out her nostrils. There was, however, one thing she could and would consume. That was the Holy Eucharist.

At the beginning of her illness, Marthe was visited by Our Blessed Mother who comforted her greatly. Sometime during the year 1928, Christ Himself appeared to her and this apparition changed her forever. This is when she decided to "offer herself over completely to God" and to "offer her sufferings in union with Him by prayer and love." She became more and more focused on Christ's Passion while becoming extremely close to Our Lady.

From the 1930s onward, Marthe's only sustenance was Christ in the Eucharist. No food or water would ever pass her lips. On Fridays, when she received Holy Communion, she would relive the Passion of Christ. At first it was spiritually but then it became physical. Marthe was visibly imprinted with the stigmata. God had included her among the select such as St. Francis, St. Catherine of Siena and St. Padre Pio.

As the triduum of Our Lord's Passion, Death and Resurrection took place within Marthe, the blood would be wet and fresh on Friday, dry on Saturday and gone on Sunday. Indeed, Marthe Robin experienced the Holy Eucharist in an extraordinary way. This would be her life until she died in 1981, a period of 51 years.

Even though Marthe never finished grade school she was able to counsel many who visited her with great words of wisdom. She possessed an overflowing sense of compassion and had an exceptional memory. During her lifetime it is estimated that more than 100,000 people visited her and received guidance from her. She honored thousands of prayer requests and her influence reached far beyond her small bedroom.

Pope Francis declared Marthe Robin venerable on Nov. 7, 2014. Today an average of 40,000 people a year visit and pray at the home where Venerable Marthe lived and died. Marthe was quoted as saying, "I want to cry out to those who ask me if I eat, that I eat more than them, for I am fed by the Eucharist of the blood and flesh of Jesus. I would like to tell them that it is they who arrest and block the effects of this food in themselves."

This account of Marthe Robin was taken from the internet. We pray that these well-documented miracles will be a powerful inspiration in strengthening our faith in the doctrine of the Real Presence of Christ in the Eucharist. Please share these facts with those who do not believe.

THIRTEEN

From the Cross to the Resurrection

Then Jesus told his disciples, "If any man would come after me, let him deny himself and take up his cross and follow me" (Mt. 16: 24)

A parishioner came to the Rectory, in her usual upbeat spirit, to do preparatory work on our upcoming festivities. With a beaming smile she said to me, "Father, today is my tenth anniversary." I was immediately aware of the awesome miracle that took place ten years earlier that changed her life and opened my eyes to a deeper understanding of the mystery of the Cross.

It was in May 1991 that we were celebrating a Mass that included the rite of Baptism in the Holy Spirit. After Mass we invited those who needed prayer to come forward. This lady, who was suffering from MS, happened to be there and came forward for prayer. For some time now the Lord had been inviting her to embrace her affliction and offer it at the Cross. That night she decided to accept this invitation and willingly walk the way of the Cross, in imitation of her Savior. The following morning she woke up and could not believe what she was experiencing: Her condition of MS had been completely healed.

When she called me later to relate the good news, I was stunned. Never before had I been witness to or read of such an amazing healing. I had been in the healing ministry for about sixteen years. People from all walks of life had come to me for prayer for healing. In all cases people were asking to have their crosses removed. It never once occurred to me to invite them to embrace their crosses as part of the journey to healing. I would now take a long hard look at my ministry; I would revisit the mystery and wisdom of the Cross.

The lie that moved our First Parents to sin was Satan's words, "You will not die; for God knows that when you eat of it your eyes will be opened, and you will be like God, knowing good and evil" (Gen 3:4). It was the blinding power of pride that drove the Devil to rebel in the first place so that he could become a god, independent and power-wielding. But his rebellion cost his eternal happiness. He would forever hate God and everything of God. Satan had his day, however, in the Garden of Eden.

In succumbing to disobedience, our First Parents lost original justice. Heaven was closed to them and their descendants. Cosmos was replaced by chaos — order by disorder. Enter death, suffering, and evils of every description. Yet God had another plan in mind. He would send His Son who would restore by obedience what was lost by disobedience. St. Paul puts it this way, "For just as through the disobedience of one person the many were made sinners, so through the obedience of one the many will be made righteous" (Rom. 5:19). The antidote to sin — the rebellious rejection of the authority of God in quest of godhead — would be for Christ the emptying of Himself of the Heavenly estate and taking on the form of a slave (Phil. 2:5-11).

The instrument of restoration that Jesus would choose was the Cross. He made this clear to His disciples time and time again. "Then he began to teach them that the Son of Man must undergo great suffering, and be rejected by the elders, the chief priests, and the scribes, and be killed, and after three days rise again" (Mk. 8:31). He likened the journey of the Cross to the process that takes place in nature. "Very truly, I tell you, unless a grain of wheat falls into the earth and dies, it remains just a single grain; but if it dies, it bears much fruit. Those who love their life, lose it, and those who hate their life in this world will keep it for eternal life" (Jn.12:24-25).

The Cross would now become the Tree of Life. The fruit of the tree in the Garden brought death. Death on the Cross would bring life eternal. Jesus' determination to go to the Cross is prophesied in Isaiah:

> The Lord God has opened my ear, and I was not rebellious, I turned not backward. I gave my back to the smiters, and my cheeks to those who pulled out the beard; I hid not my face from shame and spitting. For the Lord God helps me; therefore I have not been confounded; therefore I have set my face like a flint, and I know that I shall not be put to shame (Is. 5:4-7).

As Jesus went to the Cross, He led the way, in humble obedience, to the utter helplessness of the crucifixion. It is in this total obedience that Jesus stands out in stark contrast to sin. It is because of this humble obedience that God the Father would raise Jesus up in glory. The Letter to the

Hebrews points out, "Son though he was, he learned obedience from what he suffered; and when he was made perfect, he became the source of eternal salvation for all who obey him" (Heb. 5:8-9). And again, "For this reason, when he came into the world, he said: 'Sacrifice and offering you did not desire, but a body you prepared for me; holocausts and sin offerings you took no delight in. Then I said, as is written of me in the scroll, Behold, I come to do your will, O God'" (Heb. 10:5-6).

As Jesus entered glory through the Cross, He opened the way for us to share that glory. In Baptism we die and rise with Him. As St. Paul proclaims: "Do you not know that all of us who have been baptized into Christ Jesus were baptized into his death? Therefore we have been buried with him by baptism into death, so that, just as Christ was raised from the dead by the glory of the Father, so we too might walk in newness of life" (Rom. 6:3-4). Henceforth, the disciples of Jesus will walk the path of the Cross to glory.

St. Paul is undoubtedly a powerful witness to the Risen Christ. He relates how he tried to destroy the Church for he believed it to be an aberration. It was on one of his missions of destruction that he encountered the Risen Lord. When he was baptized his life was transformed. He was filled with the Holy Spirit and aglow with the presence of Christ. Yet he will always connect the reality of the Cross to Resurrection. "I have been crucified with Christ; and it is no longer I who live, but it is Christ who lives in me. And the life I now live in the flesh I live by faith in the Son of God, who loved me and gave himself for me" (Gal. 2:19-20). Life in Christ begins at Baptism where our souls are transformed with the new life of grace. The Holy Trinity has come to life in us.

When he wrote to the Corinthians, Paul would emphasize that his power came not from worldly wisdom or rhetorical savvy. These, he said, would deprive the cross of its power — that is its power to save: "For Christ did not send me to baptize but to preach the gospel, and not with eloquent wisdom, lest the cross of Christ be emptied of its power" (1Cor. 1:17). Rather, the cross is now to be the standard by which all allegiance will be judged.

The cross will henceforth be at the heart of Paul's preaching. On the surface this would seem strange. As an evangelist, he would literally be announcing "good news." Yet to the culture of Paul's time the cross was horrendously "bad news."

It was the weak and the powerless, slaves, and unruly criminals who were crucified in the Roman Empire. The cross was the most savage instrument of torture and death conceived by man. Cicero called it "the most cruel and disgusting penalty." Jews in Corinth, familiar with Deuteronomy, would have identified the crucified one as afflicted by God's curse. "When someone is convicted of a crime punishable by death and is executed, and you hang him on a tree, his corpse must not remain all night upon the tree; you shall bury him that same day, for anyone hung on a tree is under God's curse" (Deut. 21:22-23). Thus St. Paul would declare to another community: "Christ redeemed us from the curse of the law by becoming a curse for us – for it is written, 'Cursed is everyone who hangs on a tree' – in order that in Christ Jesus the blessing of Abraham might come to the Gentiles, so that we might receive the promise of the Spirit through faith" (Gal. 3:13-14).

Little wonder then that the mystery of the Cross was so hard to digest. Today it is no different. When we encounter Jesus' assertion, "whoever does not take up the cross and follow me is not worthy of me" (Mt. 10:38), we are stricken by its apparent harshness. Yet the discovery of the wisdom of the Cross has brought revolutionary breakthroughs.

What is this wisdom? It is the great paradox. If we want to live, we must die. If we want to be free, we must surrender our wills to Christ and become slaves for the Gospel. If we want to be empowered, we must surrender control and embrace helplessness. If we want our burdens eased, we must take His yoke upon or shoulders for He says: "My yoke is easy, and my burden is light" (Mt. 11:30). If we want resurrection and blessing we must embrace our cross. If we want to reach our fullest potential, we must become as little children. The image of a child coming to a loving parent, with hands raised in helplessness and in trust, is one of the most powerful examples to me of the wisdom of the Cross. The image of the crucifix will be for Christians the everlasting symbol inviting us to recognize our helplessness and to come to God our Abba-Father, so as to enter the embrace of His infinite love.

Perhaps one of the greatest examples of the wisdom of the cross has ironically emerged in an association that has no Church affiliation — Alcoholics Anonymous. The Twelve Steps take their inspiration from the Cross. The first step is the embrace of helplessness. The dawn begins to break on the long night of addiction when addicts acknowledge their helplessness in overcoming this habit. The second step is to acknowledge a Higher Power who can lead them to sobriety, and third to turn one's will and one's life over to God's care. For a fuller detail of the twelve steps, check the internet. What you will see is the wisdom of the Gospel as it deals with personal sin and inner brokenness, forgiveness of offenders, and of self. For progress to continue, active participation must continue in community involvement, and ministry with fellow addicts, family, co-workers, and co-worshipers.

For us, the story of the two thieves crucified with Christ illustrates the power of the cross to bless or to curse – depending how we receive it. Both men had identical sentences. Both were equally close to Christ. Yet one man was lost and the other found salvation. One man cursed his cross and was consumed by it. The other embraced his cross, looked upon the face of Jesus and heard the most wonderful words that could be spoken to any mortal, "Truly I tell you, today you will be with me in Paradise" (Lk. 23:43). What is abundantly clear is this: It is not what happens to us in life that ultimately matters. It is what we do with it that matters. In my ministry with people now I make this very clear. By and large people come to get rid of their crosses. I invite them to meditate on the scene at Calvary and follow the example of St. Dismas. Learning to bear the crosses of life, out of love for Jesus, in the power of the Holy Spirit, is the certain way to peace and the shortest road to healing, as so many over the years have discovered.

The Sisters of the Resurrection, who staff St. Veronica's Parish, have embossed on their professional crosses: "From the Cross and Death to Resurrection and Glory." May these words be embossed on each one of our hearts.

St. Augustine states that "the resurrection of Christ was God's supreme and totally marvelous work" (cf. Sat. Night Prayer). It is new life, exultation, joy; it is full of hope and a guarantee of eternal life to those who surrender to the lordship of Christ. It has been prophesied in the Scriptures:

> For I will take you from the nations, and gather you from all the countries, and bring you into your own land. I will sprinkle clean water upon you, and you shall be clean from all your uncleannesses, and from all your idols I will cleanse you. A new heart I will give you, and a new spirit I will put within you; and I will take out of your flesh the heart of stone and give you a heart of flesh. And I will put my spirit within you, and cause you to walk in my statutes and be careful to observe my ordinances. You shall dwell in the land which I gave to your fathers; and you shall be my people, and I will be your God (Ez. 36:24-28).

St. Paul rejoices in this new life that fulfills the prophecies of old:

> Do you not know that all of us who have been baptized into Christ Jesus were baptized into his death? We were buried therefore with him by

baptism into death, so that as Christ was raised from the dead by the glory of the Father, we too might walk in newness of life (Rom. 6:3-4).

St. Luke in the Acts of the Apostles brings us Peter's proclamation:

> They put him to death by hanging him on a tree; but God raised him on the third day and made him manifest; not to all the people but to us who were chosen by God as witnesses, who ate and drank with him after he rose from the dead. And he commanded us to preach to the people, and to testify that he is the one ordained by God to be judge of the living and the dead. To him all the prophets bear witness that everyone who believes in him receives forgiveness of sins through his name (Acts 10:39-43).

The Good News now is that we share in the riches of Jesus' death and resurrection. In Baptism we die and rise with Christ. Through our lives we continue this process of dying and rising, as we face our frailties and surrender to the mercy and love of Christ, that comes to us now through the Holy Spirit. May Jesus Risen be ever praise and glorified!

> Put on then, as God's chosen ones, holy and beloved, compassion, kindness, lowliness, meekness, and patience, forbearing one another and, if one has a complaint against another,

forgiving each other; as the Lord has forgiven you, so you also must forgive. And above all these put on love, which binds everything together in perfect harmony. And let the peace of Christ rule in your hearts, to which indeed you were called in the one body. And be thankful (Col. 3:12-15).

What a blessed invitation!

FOURTEEN

The Power of Pentecost

When the day of Pentecost had come, they were all together in one place. And suddenly a sound came from heaven like the rush of a mighty wind, and it filled all the house where they were sitting. And there appeared to them tongues as of fire, distributed and resting on each one of them. And they were all filled with the Holy Spirit and began to speak in other tongues, as the Spirit gave them utterance.

Now there were dwelling in Jerusalem Jews, devout men from every nation under heaven. And at this sound the multitude came together, and they were bewildered, because each one heard them speaking in his own language. And they were amazed and wondered, saying, "Are not all these who are speaking Galileans? And how is it that we hear, each of us in his own native language? (Acts 2:1-8).

Here in St. Luke's Acts of the Apostles, we witness the explosive event of Pentecost. The Jewish gathering of pilgrims from many nations, speaking many different languages, had gathered to celebrate the Jewish Feast of First Fruits.

Each year, Pentecost brings a new outpouring of the Holy Spirit and a new infusion of vigorous life into the ministry and mission of the Church. As we celebrate the Liturgy of the Birthday of the Church, once again we witness in faith the Risen Lord Jesus breathing the Holy Spirit upon His Church.

The Spirit who transformed the Apostles and empowered them as fearless preachers of the Gospel returns to engage the Church in a renewed mission of bold proclamation of Jesus' savings mysteries.

As we prepared to enter the new Millennium, our Holy Father, Pope John Paul II called the Church to pray for a "new springtime of Christianity" where Jesus will be proclaimed as the "key, focus and goal of all human history" (*Gaudium et Spes*, 10). That springtime could only become a reality through the workings of the Holy Spirit. Pope Paul IV made this abundantly clear in his historic document, *Evangelii Nuntiandi*, the decree on Evangelization in the Modern World: Again, let us return to his words that are so important to the work of evangelization:

> Evangelization will never be possible without the action of the Holy Spirit. The Spirit descends on Jesus of Nazareth at the moment of his baptism when the voice of the Father – "This is my beloved Son with whom I am well pleased" – manifests in an external way the election of Jesus and His mission... It is in the power of the Spirit that He returns to Galilee and begins His preaching at

Nazareth, applying to Himself the passage of Isaiah: "The Spirit of the Lord is upon me." And He proclaims: "Today this Scripture has been fulfilled." To the disciples whom he was about to send forth He says, breathing on them, "Receive the Holy Spirit"...

It is in the "consolation of the Holy Spirit" that the Church increases. The Holy Spirit is the soul of the Church. It is he who explains to the faithful the deeper meaning of the teaching of Jesus and of His mystery. It is the Holy Spirit who, today just as at the beginning of the Church, acts in every evangelizer who allows himself to be possessed and led by Him. The Holy Spirit places on His lips the words which he could not find by himself, and at the same time the Holy Spirit disposed the soul of the hearer to be open and receptive to the Good News and to the kingdom being proclaimed (75).

Our Holy Father's dream for evangelizing the world would come about only by the power of the Holy Spirit. We surely need in our time another mighty wind and tongues of fire to awaken the Church from her sleep, to burn away her fears in divine love, to empower her children as bold and committed heralds of the Gospel. I have been privileged to work with clergy, religious, and laity whose lives have been radically changed through the anointing and empowerment of the Holy Spirit. During my years as Pastor of St. Veronica Parish in Howell, NJ we introduced the Life in the Spirit Seminars and the Men's and Women's Retreats, and the fire of the Holy Spirit began to burn. Lives were transformed; dynamic ministry was born. Some of the most dynamic preachers and teachers came our way. In this process of transformation, the Holy Spirit inspired us to establish an Adoration Chapel in 1995 which was blessed by Bishop Smith on September 14th, the feast of the Exaltation of the Holy Cross. Over five hundred adorers signed up, and Eucharistic Adoration has continued through the years, twenty-four/seven. What a blessing!

Yes, the Holy Spirit is our life, He is our strength, and He is our inspiration. He is our success in every endeavor. He empowers our speech and He opens our ears to understanding. He releases our gifts and He prepares the groundwork for their use. He establishes community in the Church and is the soul of liturgical worship and all communal undertakings. Our whole being then should be immersed in the Holy Spirit. Our eternal prayer should be: "Come, O Holy Spirit, fill the hearts of the faithful. Enkindle in them the fire of your love." The document *Fanning the Flame* encourages us to seek a deeper infilling of the Holy Spirit and describes it thus,"Fuller life in the Holy Spirit, the Spirit's charismatic anointing, endows the Church with a full range of gifts. Gifts of adoration, praise, and prayer deepen the contemplative dimension of Christian faith. Gifts of service animate a life of Christian holiness committed to justice. All the charisms bring a new docility to the Holy Spirit, an expectant faith in God's saving intervention in human affairs, an enhanced zeal for the gospel, and a respect for authority in the Church" (22).

St. Paul lays out for us the variety of spiritual gifts that are the gift of Pentecost to the Church:

Now concerning spiritual gifts, brethren, I do not want you to be uninformed. You know that when you were heathen, you were led astray to dumb idols, however you may have been moved. Therefore I want you to understand that no one speaking by the Spirit of God ever says "Jesus be cursed!" and no one can say "Jesus is Lord" except by the Holy Spirit. Now there are varieties of gifts, but the same Spirit; and there are varieties of service, but the same Lord; and there are varieties of working, but it is the same God who inspires them all in everyone. To each is given the manifestation of the Spirit for the common good. To one is given through the Spirit the utterance of wisdom, and to another the utterance of knowledge according to the same Spirit, to another faith by the same Spirit, to another gifts of healing by the one Spirit, to another the working of miracles, to another prophecy, to another the ability to distinguish between spirits, to another various kinds of tongues, to another the interpretation of tongues. All these are inspired by one and the same Spirit, who apportions to each one individually as he wills. For just as the body is one and has many members, and all the members of the body, though many, are one body, so it is with Christ (1 Cor. 12:1-12).

St. John Paul II gave a concise but illuminating and inspiring catechesis on the seven gifts of the Holy Spirit in his General Audience of April 3, 1991. He defines the gifts as "exquisitely divine energies which the Holy Spirit pours in the soul" to perfect the virtues by giving the human spirit the capacity to act in a divine way. Every Christian receives these gifts according to the generous measure of God's love accommodated to their vocation and their specific individual spiritual journey. The seven gifts corresponded to the basic dynamism of the spiritual life: gifts of wisdom, knowledge, and understanding to illuminate the mind; gifts of counsel to strengthen the will; and gifts of piety and reverence that enable us to grow in a personal relationship through prayer and an upright life.

St. John Paul II gives us a summary of individual gifts as follows: The gift of wisdom enlightens the intellect for spiritual understanding, helping the Christian to understand reality from a divine perspective. The gift of understanding gives insight and interior understanding of God's Word; primary to this is that we stand under the Lordship of Jesus Christ. The gift of knowledge is supernatural capacity to grasp the content of divine revelation and to discern the things of God in one's knowledge of the world. The gift of counsel is a supernatural ability to regulate one's life and choices, no matter how difficult, in accord with the guidance of the Holy Spirit. The gift of fortitude supports the will in prompt and persevering faithfulness to God's commands in the face of great difficulties even to the point of martyrdom, not only dying for the faith, but even the more common martyrdom of illness and infirmity.

We have seen that the Holy Father would later illustrate these words by his own heroic witness of fortitude in the illness that he would endure at the end of his life. The gift of piety imparts the Holy Spirit to "direct the heart of man toward God with feelings, affections, thoughts and prayers" which expresses our relationship to the Father as his children in Jesus Christ. It also calls forth an appreciation and reverence for the Jesus in one another and in all of creation. The seventh gift of the Holy Spirit, the fear of the Lord, fills the soul with a profound respect for God's law. It is not a servile fear but a "filial fear steeped in love." The fear of the Lord is a profound reverence toward God, who has so lovingly adopted us as his children. Pope Saint John Paul concludes his catechesis on the gifts of the Holy Spirit with an exhortation to be "in tune" with the Holy Spirit whose love is manifested by his many gifts (National Service Committee Leaflet).

As we have celebrated in 2018 the 50th anniversary of the birth of charismatic renewal in the Catholic Church, we are deeply grateful to the Lord for the vast spiritual riches with which He has blessed the Church through Baptism in the Holy Spirit. During this period of time, one in ten of our Catholic brothers and sisters have experienced a deeper call to holiness, a new and experiential relationship with God whereby He now becomes Abba, Father (Gal. 4:6; Rom. 8:15). They have encountered the grandeur and power of Jesus' Lordship (1Cor. 12:3) and have experienced a new intimacy of faith in community and have been called to undertake apostolic and evangelical endeavors for the Church which was hitherto reserved to the presbyterate and religious orders. They have enjoyed the fruits of the Spirit: "If we live by the Spirit, let us also be guided by the Spirit" (Gal. 5:25) and have come to a deeper insight into the mysteries of redemption. They have found a new hunger for the Word and have been gifted with new ways of praise and worship, prophecy and discernment. They have been blessed with gifts of teaching, witnessing, healing, and other charisms for the building up of the Body of Christ. They have come to love and appreciate the Church more deeply and respect the teaching authority of the Magisterium.

Here I will add a note I received from a person who has come to experience the intimacy and power of the Spirit in her life:

> Wednesday's Mass was the most moving experience of my life. The power that rushed through my hands was so warm and strong and powerful. A heavy warm feeling was with me until noon the next day. As I shared my experience with a friend there was a rush of energy in my hands still. During your healing prayer over me, I was moved to share this power with another friend, who had been trying to get pregnant for four years. When she shared that she was two and a half months pregnant, the most intense feeling of joy filled my heart because I knew that Jesus was truly present showing His knowledge and power. How blessed I am! My family and friends have been truly touched, moved, and changed. Whatever Jesus wants of me, it is His, for now I know His perfect peace.

What a wonderful testimony from a person who has experienced the power of the Holy Spirit. It is a reminder to us that our testimonies are powerful weapons for evangelizing and bringing others into this awesome vortex of divine love.

As we celebrate Pentecost each year, let us glorify the Lord for calling us into His wonderful light and let us pray that the fire of the Holy Spirit will continue to bring new life and vigor to the Church by releasing a torrent of spiritual gifts on the Church. In this way, the Gospel will be preached with new conviction and vitality and that "springtime of Christianity" will become a bountiful harvest for the Kingdom of God.

So where did this Charismatic Renewal Movement in the Catholic Church really begin?

We can say that it started at the beginning of the twentieth century with Pope Leo XIII who consecrated the Church and the new century to the Holy Spirit.

19th Century: A Spark that Lit a Blazing Fire

Towards the end of the 19th century, God began to plant the seeds that would grow into the present-day charismatic renewal. From 1895 to 1903, Blessed Elena Guerra, foundress of the Oblate Sisters of The Holy Spirit in Italy, wrote 12 confidential letters to Pope Leo XIII, asking him to encourage greater devotion to the Holy Spirit among Catholics.

In 1897, Pope Leo XIII published an encyclical about the Holy Spirit called *Divinum Illud Munus*. He also called for the Church to pray the Novena for Pentecost at the beginning of the new century. A novena is a prayer said for nine days, which recalls how the early Christians prayed for the nine days between Christ's Ascension and the coming of the Holy Spirit on Pentecost.

On January 1, 1901, Pope Leo XIII prayed to the Holy Spirit. He sang the *Veni Creator Spiritu*s by the Holy Spirit window in St. Peter's Basilica in Rome. That same day, in Topeka, Kansas, at the Bethel College and Bible School, the Holy Spirit came upon a group of Protestants who had been praying to receive the Holy Spirit as the early Church did in Acts chapter two. Agnes Ozman prayed in tongues and people began to welcome the Holy Spirit to work in them as in the early Church with healings, miracles, deliverance, and power to effectively evangelize and help people convert to Jesus Christ. This beginning of the charismatic renewal highlights its ecumenical nature that continues to be experienced over 100 years later. The commonly shared experience of being filled with passion and love for God has been a major way that the charismatic renewal helps bring Catholics and Protestants together to build relationships and learn to recognize many common areas of Christian living.

The historic events at the beginning of the charismatic renewal are significant for unity not only among individual Christians, but also for unity in the entire worldwide Church. As seen in this historic event, the Pope's prayers resulted in an outpouring of the Holy Spirit upon Protestants. This highlights how through the Pope, God gives a special gift of apostolic covering to all Christians. The Pope is able to minister on an international level in a way that even the most well-travelled evangelists do not experience. While most pastors minister on a local level, the Pope fills a need to minister to the whole Church on a worldwide level.

This is taken from the first part of *A New Pentecost,* Patti Mansfield Gallagher's history of the Duquesne Weekend:

> The retreat of February 17-19, 1967, which I describe in my letter, has come to be known around the world as the Duquesne Weekend. It is generally accepted as the beginning of the Charismatic Renewal in the Catholic Church. This was the first event at which a group of Catholics experienced the Baptism in the Spirit and the charismatic gifts. While there may have been Catholics who were baptized in the Spirit prior to the Duquesne Weekend, this retreat began a widespread movement of Catholic Charismatic Renewal throughout the United States and around the world. I was not the only Catholic giving exuberant witness to the new outpouring of the Holy Spirit and His gifts in 1967. Through letters, phone calls, and personal visits, word was spreading like wildfire about the pentecostal experience. One of the professors who was a leader on the Duquesne Weekend reported to his friends at Notre Dame, "I don't have to believe in Pentecost, because I've seen it.

Many people who reflect on the outbreak of the Catholic Charismatic Renewal in 1967 call to mind the prayer of Pope John XXIII at the beginning of the Second Vatican Council. They see the Charismatic Renewal as a providential answer to the Holy Father's prayer for a new Pentecost:

> Renew Your wonders in this our day, as by a new Pentecost. Grant to Your Church that, being of one mind and steadfast in prayer with Mary, the Mother of Jesus, and following the lead of blessed Peter, it may advance the reign of our Divine Savior, the reign of truth and justice, the reign of love and peace. Amen.

FIFTEEN

Two Journeys – Two Worlds

March 1996 – The road from Patrick's Well, County Limerick to Mallow, was winding and unfamiliar. It was only my second time making this trip, and as I motored past lush farmlands, already displaying some of Ireland's legendary shades of green on this late-March morning, a flood of memories began to return. My last journey along this route was sixteen years earlier almost to the day, when Sister Brenda and I were returning for our mother's funeral. Mom had died peacefully at Mercy Hospital in Cork on March 20, 1980 while she was in for a check-up. Our sister, Sr. Mary B., was a nurse there for many years and, as it turned out, was a real blessing to my parents in their old age. That in itself was an irony. After I was born, my mother was told that she should have no more children since another pregnancy would seriously jeopardize her health. Five years later the child "who should not have been" was born on the Feast of Our Lady of Lourdes and was given the name Mary Bernadette. She would be with my parents in their joys and their sorrows. She was present with them through their every illness and was with both when they died. How wonderful are the ways of the Lord for those who trust in Him!

As we made our way through town and hamlet, Sister Brenda and I awakened many pleasant memories of home that centered around our beloved mother. I recalled the summer of 1979 when I last visited with her. Now, in retrospect, that visit became all the more precious and all the more poignant. One of the gifts I brought my mother was a white shoulder shawl which one of my parishioners had made for her. When I presented it to her she was overjoyed. She paused for a moment and then said jubilantly, "This is so beautiful. I will not wear it now, but will keep it for my glorious day." What a beautiful way to speak about death, I thought. My mother was a deeply spiritual and prayerful woman throughout her life. I recall her Holy Hours and other devotions, her love for the Rosary, and most especially the Eucharist. As long as I could remember, our home was consecrated to the Sacred Heart of Jesus and to the Immaculate Heart of Mary. As with most Irish homes, a red vigil light burned before the picture of the Sacred Heart to constantly remind us – and the visitor – Who it was who reigned in our home.

My mother was overjoyed that members of her family would devote their lives to the service of the Church, even though it meant seeing very little of them for the rest of her earthly life. The joyful gatherings were all too short, only to be followed by painful good-byes. Yet she never complained but always looked forward with patient longing for the next reunion.

Mom had very few worldly possessions, and what she had, she had given away prior to her death. That summer she called me to her room one day and said that she wanted me to have her crucifix with which she had prayed throughout the years. It would become my fondest possession and a daily reminder of the heritage of faith and love that she had left me. Now that she was gone to her eternal reward, the significance of the previous summer visit became all the more important. Did my mother know that it would be our last earthly reunion? Was the Lord preparing her and me for this "glorious day" that seemed to come so suddenly? At Mercy Hospital we would find her earthly remains beautifully laid out in the Convent Chapel, surrounded by family, friends, and the many Sisters of Mercy who had come to know and love her over the years. The Eucharistic celebration, before we began the journey home to Kerry, was an intensely warm and a truly joyous experience of heavenly love. This was undoubtedly the beginning of Mom's "glorious day'" that would never know ending.

She had experienced her final birth, the ultimate healing, the reunion with departed loved ones, the end of an exile, the beginning of the final purgative process that would adorn her soul for transition into Eternal Bliss. In the Eucharist we thanked the Lord for the gift that she was to us, and we lovingly surrendered her back to Him, to live in His Heart forever. Today, when I look to the Sacred Heart, I sense my mother's presence adoring and interceding. What a wonderful mystery our faith is!

When we returned home after the funeral, my Dad said, "I would like to go as Mom did." Somehow, the Lord heard his wish and prayer. Six years later, Sr. Mary B. was preparing to leave Cork City for a Conference in Dublin, when she received an interior message that said: "Return to your home in Kerry." She cancelled her trip to Dublin and went home to our Dad who was already coming close to death. She had the privilege of ministering to him and praying with him. She held his hand as he drew his last breath. How great is our God!

Now, ten years later I was retracing that journey to Cork to preach at a Charismatic Youth Conference. Over the years I had come to know some wonderful people in this City by the Lee and had occasion to speak and celebrate Mass there for the Charismatic community on a number of occasions. I felt honored that the young people had asked me to be the speaker at their conference and wondered how the Lord would use me on that special weekend.

In preparation, I called upon all my friends in faith to intercede for a powerful outpouring of the Holy Spirit upon me and on all those who would attend the Conference. For several weeks, some friends and I gathered on Tuesday afternoons at St. Mary's Mission Church in adoration and intercession before the Blessed Sacrament. People sent in encouraging and insightful words they had received in prayer that were helpful in preparing my talks. Sister Mary B. and the organizing committee were busy on the other side of the Atlantic attending to details and waiting in prayer. Now the time had finally arrived and I was coming ever nearer the beloved City of St. Finbarr which had so many special memories from the past.

Cork had over the years made its own significant contribution of great leaders to Church and State since St. Finbarr decided to make her his place of resurrection. At the present time two of her notable sons were brother

Bishops in the United States. Bishops Kevin and Raymond Boland were fellow alumni of All Hallows College in Dublin. Before I left for Ireland, I asked them both to write letters to the young people at the Conference that would be encouraging and inspirational. They graciously responded with letters that would later receive thunderous applause when read on the weekend. These beautiful letters provided a connectedness between hierarchical and lay, between the Church at home and abroad, between the missionary spirit of past generations and a new level of evangelical and spiritual fire that was now being ignited.

The new road from Mallow to Cork eased the final leg of my journey; before long I was greeting Sister Mary B. in Mayfield at her apartment, which is nestled among the city's poorer and more marginalized citizens. My sister was excited and filled with cautious enthusiasm. She shared with me the details of preparation and the air of excitement that prevailed among the organizing committee. I was happy to be back in Cork and looked forward to yet another glorious day in the marvelous plans of our God.

Before I could get too relaxed, my sister informed me that I was due at Cork Radio and Television Studios for an interview with Ger Canning, well-known sports announcer and media personality. The interview was brief and rather superficial, yet it was an important sound bite promoting the conference throughout Cork and South Munster.

The Conference was a wonderful outpouring of the Holy Spirit. The fervor of prayer and praise, the openness to the Word, and the anointed music ministry revealed the power of the Holy Spirit. The intensity of adoration before the Blessed Sacrament on Saturday night, and the powerful witnessing of young people whose lives had been transformed as they gave their hearts to Christ gave glory to God. The glorious celebration of Mass on Sunday afternoon, the rejoicing in song that continued long after Mass, and the stories of healings during the weekend all manifested to us very clearly that the Lord had indeed visited His beloved people by the Lee.

Despite the scandals that rock the Church in Ireland today and reports of widespread departures of young people from the practice of their faith, it was really encouraging to see so many young and old alike openly expressing their love for God and for His Church.

As we rejoiced together in the Lord, I recalled a section of *Evangelii Nuntiandi* that I had highlighted,

> We live in the Church in a privileged moment of the Spirit. Everywhere people are trying to know Him better, as the Scripture reveals Him. They are happy to place themselves under His inspiration. They are gathering about Him; they want to let themselves be led by Him. Now if the Spirit of God has a preeminent place in the whole life of the Church, it is in her evangelizing mission that He is most active. It is not by chance that the great inauguration of evangelization took place on the morning of Pentecost, under the inspiration of the Holy Spirit (75).

From this experience, it was abundantly clear to me that Ireland needs what every other local Church needs – a new revival in the Holy Spirit, a new Pentecost. The daily media blitz of Church scandals could not dull the force of the Spirit that rocked Neptune Stadium that weekend. The Lord is raising up some wonderful young people in Ireland whose depth and sincerity of faith is truly inspiring. If the nation as a whole follows the lead of the Spirit, Ireland will become once again the Island of Saints and Scholars and will feature boldly in bringing the Good News to a world that is mired in sin and darkness. My two journeys to Cork were in a way symbolic of the two Irish worlds that I have known. I grew up in an Ireland that was rich in active faith, strong in family and community life, protected by mores that were prized and respected by all, sharing an identity that was undoubtedly Catholic where history, culture, and religion intersected. The Ireland I grew up in was spiritually and culturally rich but materially poor. Hard work and frugal living combined to make ends meet. This was the Ireland that my mother represented; it was an Ireland that was quickly changing. With modernization, industrialization, entry into the European Community, a media that became enveloped in the modernistic, hedonistic and decidedly anti-Christian worldview, and an affluence that Ireland had not known before, the face of Ireland would change dramatically.

The dragnet of prosperity brought with it all the pitfalls of modern society which would now serve as corrosive agents on the spirit of young and not-so-young alike. We would now see major drops in Church attendance and in vocations to priesthood and religious life, increases in crime, drug and other addictions, marital infidelity and break-up, and sexual permissiveness. Now we would see a powerful lobby clamoring for divorce and abortion. To top it off, clerical and other scandals would light the airwaves and bring a new depth of anger, disillusionment, cynicism and despair to a Church already reeling from a hedonistic invasion.

This was the backdrop for my second trip from Shannon to Cork. It was into this arena that the Holy Spirit would descend once again and bring new life, joy, healing, and a burst of enthusiasm for the Risen Christ and for His Gospel. This was the renewed Church that the Holy Spirit has been carefully restoring since Pope Leo XIII dedicated the twentieth century to Him. With the Vatican Council the Church would reflect on her nature and purpose and recognize that she was missionary at heart. She was called to bring the Good News of Christ's transforming love to the nations.

Theologian Father Avery Dulles describes this evolution.

> With Vatican II a major shift took place. The Catholic Church in a true sense became evangelical. The Council spoke frequently of the gospel (in Latin, *evangelium*, 157 times) and of evangelization (31 times). It taught that every Christian has a responsibility to evangelize.
>
> Paul VI followed this up in many ways. He took the name of Paul in honor of the apostle to the Gentiles and engaged in long apostolic journeys to distant continents. At the climax of his pontificate...he composed his great apostolic exhortation, *Evangelii Nuntiandi(Evangelization in the Modern World*, 1975). In this he described

evangelization as the deepest identity of the Church, which exists, as he put it, in order to evangelize. Pope John Paul II has carried this evangelical shift further. Summarizing the main orientation of his pontificate he declared in Mexico City on May 6, 1990, "The Lord and master of history and of our destinies has wished my pontificate to be that of a pilgrim pope of evangelization, walking down the roads of the world, bringing to all people the message of salvation" (*Evangelizing Theology: First Things,* March, 1996).

While we often complain about the ills of humanity and the ills of the Church, and are at a loss to find a remedy, let us remember that the answer is the Holy Spirit. Let us recall again the words of Pope Paul VI in *Evangelii Nuntiandi,*

> It is in the "consolation of the Holy Spirit" that the Church increases. The Holy Spirit is the soul of the Church. It is He who explains to the faithful the deep meaning of the teaching of Jesus and His mystery. It is the Holy Spirit who, today just as in the beginning of the Church, acts in every evangelizer who allows himself to be possessed and led by Him (75).

Thanks to the Holy Spirit, flowing from the heart of Christ, that all our work was made possible. Thanks also for the wonderful people who assisted my many endeavors and cooperated so wholeheartedly in all of the ministries and projects that we undertook together. Many have already gone before us to be with the Lord. They now await our joining them in sharing the glory of Heaven forever. We pray that this reading from the Feast of All Saints will encourage us to continue our journey home to our Father's House and bring many, many souls along with us.

The reading for the feast of All Saints is taken from a sermon by St. Bernard, Abbot. He was given the title of Mellifluous (honey-flowing) Doctor, so gifted was he as a preacher and author. So we will share some of his words for our reflection as we come to the close.

> Why should our praise and glorification, or even the celebration of this feastday mean anything to the saints? What do they care about earthly honors when their heavenly Father honors them by fulfilling the faithful promise of the Son? What does our commendation mean to them? The saints have no need of honor from us; neither does our devotion add the slightest thing to what is theirs. Clearly, if we venerate their memory, it serves us, not them. But I tell you what I think of them, I feel myself inflamed by a tremendous yearning.

> Calling the saints to mind inspires, or rather arouses in us, above all else, a longing to enjoy their company, so desirable in itself. We long to share the citizenship or heaven, to dwell in the spirit of the blessed, to join the assembly of patriarchs, the ranks of the prophets, the counsel of the apostles, the great host of martyrs, the noble company of

confessors and the choirs of virgins. In short, we long to be united in happiness with all the saints....

Come, brothers and sisters, let us at length spur ourselves on. We must rise again with Christ, we must seek the world which is above and set our mind on the things of heaven. Let us long for those who are longing for us, hasten to those who are waiting for us. We should not only want to be with the saints, we should also hope to possess their happiness. While we desire to be in their company, we must also seek to share in their glory. Do not imagine that there is anything harmful in such an ambition as this; there is no danger in setting our hearts on such glory. When we commemorate the saints we are inflamed with another yearning: that Christ our life may also appear to us as he appeared to them and that we one day share in his glory.

With these words of the Mellifluous Doctor, I bring these chapters to a close. I pray that they will be a source of inspiration and increase your longing to be one day in the company of all the great saints in heaven. If you find comfort and inspiration in them, feel free to pass them on to family, friends, and perhaps someone who is confused and hungry for God. I wrote them because I was inspired by many great preachers, authors, and witnesses to the power of the Gospel.

Thanks to the Holy Spirit, flowing from the heart of Christ, that all our work was made possible. Thanks also to the wonderful people who encouraged and helped in putting these chapters together and reviewing the text.

Without their professional help this work would have been impossible. They all have let their light shine for me in every endeavor along the journey to our Father's House.

> In the same way, let your light shine before others, so that they may see your good works and give glory to your Father in heaven (Mt. 5:16).

BIBLIOGRAPHY

Bonaventure. *The Journey of the Mind to God*. Hackett Publishing Company, 1990.

Bro, Bernard.*The Little Way: The Spirituality of Therese of Lisieux.*Alba House, 2014.

Brown, Raymond. *The Churches the Apostles Left Behind*. Paulist Press, 1984.

Catechism of the Catholic Church. https://www.vatican.va/archive/ENG0015/_INDEX.HTM

Cordes, Paul Josef. Call to Holiness: Reflections on the Catholic Charismatic Renewal. Liturgical Press, 1997.

Daniel-Rops, Henri. *The Saints of Ireland*. Irish American Cultural Institute, 1974.

Dulles, Avery. "Evangelizing Theology." *First Things*, March 1996.

Dulles, Avery. *John Paul II and the New Evangelization*. Ignatius Press, 1995.

Erikson, Erik. *Identity and the Life Cycle*. W.W. Norton & Co. (1958-1980).

Gallagher, Patti Mansfield. *As by a New Pentecost: The Dramatic Beginning of the Catholic Charismatic Renewal*. Franciscan University Press, 1992.

Hahn, Scott. *The Lamb's Supper: The Mass as Heaven on Earth*. Doubleday, 1999.

John Paul II. *Veritatis Splendor* (The Splendor of Truth). http://www.vatican.va/content/john-paul-ii/en/encyclicals/documents/hf_jp-ii_enc_06081993_veritatis-splendor.html

Kelsey, Morton. *Psychology, Medicine, and Christian Healing*. Harper & Row, 1988.

Kowalska, Maria Faustina. *Diary of St. Faustina: Divine Mercy in My Soul*. Marian Helpers, 1987.

McDonnell, Kilian. Fanning the Flame: What Does Baptism in the Holy Spirit Have to Do with Christian Initiation. Michael Glazier, 1991.

McKenna, Briege. *Miracles Do Happen*. Veritas Publications, 1987.

McManus, Seumas. *The Story of the Irish Race*. Devin-Adair Company, 1969.

Paul VI. Evangelii Nuntiandi (Evangelization in the Modern World). http://www.vatican.va/content/paul-vi/en/apost_exhortations/documents/hf_p-vi_exh_19751208_evangelii-nuntiandi.html

Ratzinger, Joseph. *Ratzinger Report: An Exclusive Interview on the State of the Church*. Ignatius Press, 1985.

Scanlon, Michael. *Let the Fire Fall*. Franciscan University Press, 1997.

Tesoriero, Ron. *Reason to Believe*. 2007.

Kempis, Thomas à. *The Imitation of Christ*. TAN Books, 2013.

Therese of Lisieux. *Story of a Soul*. ICS Publications, 1996.